Y327.73047 G61E   2205225
GOODE, STEPHEN.
THE END OF detente?: U.S.-SOVIET
RELATIONS

THE END OF DÉTENTE?

U.S.-SOVIET RELATIONS

BY STEPHEN GOODE

A GROLIER COMPANY

FRANKLIN WATTS
New York/London/Toronto/Sydney/1981
AN IMPACT BOOK

FOR MY FRIEND, ERNIE HARPER

Library of Congress Cataloging in Publication Data

Goode, Stephen.
The end of détente?

"An Impact book."
Bibliography: p.
Includes index
Summary: Examines the relationship between the
United States and the Soviet Union, the "cold war,"
and the resultant détente and its problems.
1. United States — Foreign relations —
Soviet Union — Juvenile literature.
2. Soviet Union — Foreign relations —
United States — Juvenile literature.
3. Détente — Juvenile literature.
[1. United States —
Foreign relations — Soviet Union.
2. Soviet Union — Foreign relations — United
States.   3. Détente]   I. Title.
E183.8.S65G66   327.73047   81-11370
ISBN 0-531-04334-7   AACR2

CONTENTS

2205225

INTRODUCTION

This book is about the relationship between the United States and the Soviet Union. For almost forty years, that relationship has been at the center of world affairs. America and the USSR are "superpowers" whose size and strength dwarf that of all other nations, past or present. Both countries possess large nuclear arsenals capable of widespread destruction. Both have large armies and modern, sophisticated weapons.

The Soviet Union and the United States are rivals. Their relationship is antagonistic and often bitter. It has, at times, broken out into limited war to be followed by periods of limited peace. In the years following World War II, Walter Lippmann, the foremost American journalist and political commentator of his time, popularized the term "cold war" in describing the Soviet-American rivalry. The historian John Lukacs has called it "a cold peace." Both names are accurate and convey the tension, misunderstanding, and resentment that characterize Soviet-American relations.

In this book we shall look at the cold war and discuss its major events. One area of chief concern, however, will be recent history. In the early 1970s, the two nations attempted to establish their relationship on a new basis and come to a new understanding, called détente, that would make the occurrence of a major war less likely. The attempt failed, but its story is nevertheless important.

CHAPTER ONE
THE
SOVIET-AMERICAN RIVALRY

*Of all historical problems, the nature of national
character is the most difficult and the most important.*

Henry Adams
(noted American historian and author)

The word détente is a French word and was borrowed from
that language when French was the standard language of
diplomacy and international affairs. Originally, it referred to
the release of the strained string of the crossbow and the dis-
charge of the arrow. The French still use the word to define the
trigger of a firearm, but détente has also acquired a more general meaning. It is used to signify a calming and relaxation of
tension; in medicine, "detensive" drugs are employed to reduce
high blood pressure. The word used in Russian to describe
détente, *razriadka,* has similar origins and can mean an "un-
winding" and a release from stress and strain.

Since the time of the Russian Revolution of October
1917, a state of tension and rivalry has existed between the
United States and the Soviet Union. On occasion—during the
Berlin Crisis of 1948 and the Cuban Missile Crisis of 1962,
to cite only two examples—this tension has threatened to break
out into war. But at other times there have been periods of
relaxation, when the USSR and the United States have seemed
on the verge of a new and improved understanding.

These periods of relaxation and relative calm are known as periods of détente. Since 1945, historians have noted four such periods. The first came in 1954, one year after the death of Stalin, and led to a "summit meeting" in Geneva, Switzerland, attended by American leaders, leaders of the Soviet Union, and other foreign statesmen. The second and third periods came in 1959 and the early sixties and resulted in similar high level meetings. The fourth, which is the subject of this book, began in the early seventies and was by far the most wide-ranging and significant.

In diplomatic terms, détente lies somewhere between a "normalization of relations" and genuine rapprochement or cooperation. When two nations agree to normalize relations with each other, they exchange ambassadors and establish the basic requirements necessary to diplomacy. Deep enmities may still divide them, but they nevertheless decide to establish channels of communication in an attempt to settle their differences in traditional patterns, short of war. Rapprochement, on the other hand, is a "coming together" and "an establishment or state of cordial relations." Past differences and quarrels are dismissed or forgotten and the two nations find common interests and purposes in their foreign policies. A state of harmony or *entente* can then be said to exist.

Normalization of the relationship between the Soviet Union and the United States took place in 1933, fifteen years after the Russian Revolution when America had withdrawn official recognition of the USSR. The Russian and American embassies were reopened in Washington and Moscow, and the stage was set for the turbulence and upheaval that have characterized the Soviet-American connection since that time. Rapprochement, however, has proved impossible, except perhaps for the period of Soviet and American cooperation during World War II when the two countries were united in their efforts to crush Germany, Italy, and Japan.

Rapprochement has proved impossible for two reasons. First, the United States and the Soviet Union represent profoundly opposing views of the world. From the time of the Russian Revolution, the USSR has regarded itself as the "home" of communism and as the champion of a political, economic, and social system—Marxism-Leninism—that would eventually sweep the world. At the same time, the United States has regarded itself as the defender of individualism and democracy and the enemy of all forms of dictatorship. The ideological gulf that separates the two nations is enormous and has made it difficult for them to live together without friction, misunderstanding, and bitter suspicion.

The second reason for the enmity between the United States and the Soviet Union arises from the natural antipathy two great powers and rivals will feel for each other. Throughout history, strong, ambitious states have been antagonists and have competed with one another for power, prestige, and domination. In the ancient world, Sparta and Athens vied for control of Greece. Modern times have witnessed the rivalries of France and Germany, Great Britain and France, and many others. The Soviet-American antagonism is merely a repetition of an old theme—rivalry between great powers—now cloaked in the ideological garments of communism and capitalism.

Given these basic antagonisms between the United States and the Soviet Union, it is not surprising that rapprochement has been out of the question. The best the two nations have achieved in their cold war has been détente. But even détente, as we shall see, has been impossible to maintain. The first three détentes were short-lived and ended in renewed hostility. The fourth lasted longer, but suffered a similar fate.

U.S. AND SOVIET VIEWS
OF EACH OTHER

In both countries, much has been written about the Soviet-American rivalry. Each year thousands of books, magazine and journal articles, and government position papers add to the tons of information already available. But the process of understanding has been arduous and difficult, and has reflected the deep divisions that separate the two societies and peoples. Blinded by its own philosophy and attitudes, each has found it hard to look at the other clearly and without prejudice.

Take, for example, the two views of Soviet society generally accepted in the United States. On the one hand, the

Soviet Union is seen as a monolithic state, totally in control of its people and actively—and successfully—pursuing its own interests throughout the world. According to this view, the USSR is efficient, effective, and dangerous, a superpower that has already established a vast empire and that plans to add to this empire in the future by any available means.

On the other hand, the Soviet Union is frequently pictured as a place where "nothing works." Soviet industry is described as backward and inept and the Soviet economy as weak and incapable of satisfying the needs of its own citizens. Surely an accurate assessment of the Soviet Union would lie somewhere between these two views. But an exaggerated fear of Soviet military capabilities and an exaggerated contempt for the economic failures of communism have distorted the true image of the Soviet Union in American eyes.

Soviet understanding of the United States is likewise deeply flawed. Many Soviet experts on the United States appear incapable of picturing America with any degree of precision or accuracy. Professor Robert Byrnes of the University of Indiana, who has known many Soviet experts on the United States, notes that "they work on a mental frequency that will just not pick up American signals," even after they have spent a year in the United States, and that they have little comprehension of "what makes us tick."

There are two reasons why this is so. It is difficult for any individual from one society and culture genuinely to understand another, and when the two cultures and societies are as dissimilar as the United States and the Soviet Union, the problem of genuine understanding becomes more severe. But Soviet experts have an additional problem to overcome in their attempt to understand America, and that problem is ideology.

Most Soviet experts, if they achieve success in the Soviet · diplomatic world, are "good Communists." They have been rigorously trained in Marxism-Leninism and accept its view of history and society. Their understanding of Marxism is often subtle and complex, but it frequently prevents them from acquiring an accurate picture of the United States.

Often an American reader of the Soviet newspaper *Pravda* is amazed by what passes as accurate reporting. In

1974, for example, *Pravda* carried a story by Gennadii Vasil-kev which maintained that it is quite common in the United States under the free enterprise system for babies to be sold like cars, refrigerators, or any other product. Other writers emphasize and distort aspects of American life—like unemployment or race relations—that seem to "prove" the Marxist notion that capitalism produces decadent societies.

But there is a more sinister side to the role ideology plays in the Soviet perception of the United States. In 1946, Clark Clifford warned President Truman in a secret special report that the Soviet government was "isolated, largely ignorant of the outside world," and "blinded by adherence to Marxist dogma." A year later, Soviet expert George Kennan* wrote in *Foreign Affairs* that Communist ideology taught Soviet leaders "that the outside world was hostile and that it was their duty eventually to overthrow the political forces beyond their borders."

Thus, ideology blinds the Soviet Union at two levels. It gives Soviet writers a means to reprove America for its short-comings, making those shortcomings seem far worse than they are. At the same time it gives Soviet leaders reason to believe that the West has but one overriding goal: the destruction of communism. On the one side, ideology feeds Soviet ignorance of American ways by giving Soviet writers preconceived ideas of what the United States is like. On the other, it increases Soviet aggressiveness and distrust by giving Soviet leaders an enemy that must be overcome if communism is to survive and thrive. In both cases, ideology only adds to cold war misunderstanding and division.

A DIFFERENCE IN HISTORY

The inability of the Soviet Union and the United States to understand the other's society has been aggravated by the very

---

* George Kennan is noted for his long and distinguished career as a diplomat and scholar. During the formative years of the cold war, he was on the policy planning staff of the State Department in Washington, D.C.; he has also served as ambassador to the Soviet Union and as ambassador to Yugoslavia. He is the author of many fine studies of Soviet-American relations and a member of the Institute of Advanced Studies at Princeton.

different histories the two nations have experienced. For more than a century after its creation, the United States was isolated from the rest of the world and allowed to develop without foreign intervention. The Atlantic Ocean separated America from the conflicts and troubles of Europe.

America's first major involvement in world affairs came during World War I. But after the war, the nation rapidly reduced its commitments abroad. The first postwar President, Warren Harding, was elected on a platform that promised a "return to normalcy." It was during World War II and after that the United States shed its traditional isolationism and assumed a role as leader of the non-Communist nations.

This role, however, was very new and did not come easily. The tradition of isolationism remained strong. In times of crisis, like the Vietnam War, it caused Americans to want to withdraw from commitment and retreat into themselves. At other times, it may have increased America's cold war desire for total military and economic superiority. Americans felt uncomfortable unless their very strength isolated them from all foreign threat, just as the Atlantic had isolated them.

The Soviet Union, on the other hand, has lived in anything but isolation. From earliest times, the country has been subjected to numerous invasions. In the thirteenth century, the Mongols under Genghis Khan invaded Russia from the East and laid waste its countryside. Later came German and Swedish armies. In 1812, the French Army under Napoleon invaded Russia and eventually burned Moscow, but they were defeated by the severity of the Russian winter.

In our own century, Russia suffered humiliating defeat at the hands of the Japanese in 1905, and was twice invaded by Germany, once in World War I and again in World War II. Both wars with Germany were extremely devastating, even calamitous. The first ravaged the nation and resulted in the revolution that brought the Communists to power. The second war, against Hitler, nearly ended in Russia's defeat. Some experts estimate that nearly twenty million Soviet citizens, civilians as well as soldiers, died in that conflict.

This history of repeated invasions has fostered in Russians a deep fear and mistrust of foreigners. It has likewise fostered an understandable desire for security and the need to create a world where the Soviet Union would be free of the fear of invasion. A nation that has suffered so greatly at the hands of others must regard its own defensive posture with deep concern and vigilance.

THE PROBLEM OF INFERIORITY

Another factor that has complicated the Soviet-American relationship is fear of inferiority, first in the Soviet attitude toward the United States and lately in America's attitude toward Russia. Marxism may teach that communism will eventually be victorious and that the capitalist world will collapse under the weight of its own "inner contradictions," but, meanwhile, the fact of American technological and economic superiority cannot be denied. Soviet writers may endlessly condemn America's shortcomings, but they cannot conceal envy of her wealth and achievements.*

American society fed its people better than Russia fed hers and gave them far more of the benefits of modern civilization—cars, refrigerators, and so on. America seemed to possess a vitality and energy that could not be transplanted or cultivated in the Soviet Union. American workers were more productive than Soviet workers, and American agriculture so outpaced Soviet agriculture that the two could be compared only with extreme embarrassment for the Soviet government. In spite of repeated boasts from Soviet leaders that the Soviet economy would soon overtake the economies of the West, it has never been able to do so. As an important member of the Soviet Central Committee told an American diplomat in the mid-1970s, the United States "is a creative society. We are an uncreative society."

---

* Modern Soviet feelings of inferiority coupled with the belief that communism is the wave of the future have their parallels in earlier Russian history. From the time of Peter the Great in the early eighteenth century to the present, Russians were embarrassed and concerned about their country's backwardness. At the same time, there was also a strong belief that Russian values were superior to foreign values and that Russian Christianity was the only true faith.

Soviet feelings of inferiority are long-standing; American feelings of inferiority are newer. Until recently, most Americans regarded the moral, political, and economic superiority of the United States as without question. America was an "open" and free society; the Soviet Union was "closed" and tyrannical. The United States openly gave of its wealth and resources to defend and support weak nations; the Soviet Union invaded and enslaved.

During the 1960s and early 1970s, however, these beliefs were profoundly challenged. The long war in Vietnam deeply divided the nation. The New Left called traditional American values into question. The Watergate affair revealed corruption and dishonesty at the highest levels of government and, by 1972, inflation and unemployment had begun to play havoc with the American economy.

Political observers wondered if these events had undermined the will and determination of the United States to carry out its role as leader of the non-Communist world. They wondered, too, if the national unity and sense of purpose that had characterized America since World War II had dissolved. Was the United States moving into a new period of isolationism when it would withdraw from its commitments abroad? Would America's loss of will and unity allow the Soviet Union to move far ahead on all fronts in the superpower rivalry?

Russian fears of inferiority have played a large part in the Soviet Union's drive for economic improvement and military strength. American fears of inferiority have caused the United States in recent years to reassess its strengths and weaknesses and attempt to regain the will and determination many said had been lost. In both cases, however, these feelings have made the Soviet-American relationship more difficult and hazardous, because neither nation can deal comfortably with the other from a position of weakness or inferiority.

THE ORIGIN OF
THE MISUNDERSTANDING

From the beginning, the relationship between the United States and the Soviet Union has been marked by the rivalries, the ignorance of each other's history, and the mingled feelings of superiority and inferiority mentioned above. When the Bolsheviks seized power in Russia in October, 1917, writes George F. Kennan, "American opinion-makers were poorly prepared to understand either the meaning or the implications of the event." Russian study programs were almost nonexistent in the United States, and the American government, which had only recently entered World War I, was inclined to look upon the Russian Revolution as an event inspired by German agents hoping to remove Russia from the war.

This interpretation had some small basis in fact. Vladimir Lenin, the revolutionary leader, had been taken from exile in Switzerland and transported to Russia in a sealed railroad car by the Germans. The purpose of his removal to Russia had been the hope that once in his homeland, Lenin would foment revolution, weaken the Russian war effort, and allow Germany to concentrate on the war on the Western front. Lenin himself was not a German agent, nor were his fellow revolutionaries, but the United States, perceiving them as pro-German, refused to recognize the new regime.

This initial misunderstanding was followed by deeper problems and resentments. During the civil war that raged in Russia following the Revolution, the United States sent troops to join British and French troops in the far north of Russia and eastern Siberia. The reason behind the dispatch of the American troops is not clear. No American interest was involved, and President Woodrow Wilson had only reluctantly agreed to send them after pressure from British and French leaders.

The President insisted that there was to be no "intervention" in Russia and no fighting with the Bolsheviks. The American troops were to aid Czech prisoners-of-war in Siberia and "to guard military stores and make it safe for Russian forces to come together in organized bodies in the north." Furthermore, the American force was to be limited to seven thousand. But the war soon got out of hand and American troops ended up fighting the Bolshevik troops—in a war that had never been declared and against an army not regarded as an enemy. Secretary of War Newton Baker later said that the situation "will always illustrate the eccentricities of a remote and irrational emanation from the central madness of a warring world."

To the young revolutionary government in Moscow, however, the presence of American and other foreign troops on Russian soil could mean only one thing: the capitalist nations were out "to strangle Bolshevism in its cradle." On revolutionary posters throughout Russia, the Western soldiers were pictured as the puppets of corrupt and monstrous capitalism, whose only purpose was the destruction of the Revolution and all its achievements.

But if the presence of foreign troops in Russia angered the revolutionaries, the steady flow of Communist propaganda that came from the new regime angered and enraged the West and particularly the United States. Never before had Americans heard their country denounced as a center of reaction and as the enemy of freedom and justice. Never before had they heard the leaders of a large and potentially powerful nation speak of the inevitable collapse of every non-Communist country and the triumph of a philosophy called Marxism.

There can be no doubt that the propaganda was much less dangerous than it sounded. Russia had been extremely weakened by the war and the Revolution and was in no position to challenge the West. In large part, the purpose behind the propaganda was to create unity among the Russian people by giving them a new cause—Communism—to rally around. But at the same time, the virulence and bitterness of the propaganda was provocative and disquieting.

By 1919 and 1920, the first great "red scare," or anti-Communist hysteria, struck the United States. Exaggerated fears of Communist activity in America caused many Americans to believe that radicals of any sort were dangerous and "undesirable." Illegal raids approved by the attorney general of the United States, Alexander Mitchell Palmer, led to the arrest and deportation of thousands of aliens who were no more radical than the attorney general himself.

On August 10, 1920, Secretary of State Bainbridge Colby sent a note to the Italian government that outlined America's attitude toward the Soviet regime. "It is not possible," he wrote, "for the Government of the United States to recognize the present rulers of Russia as a government with which the relations common to friendly governments can be maintained." Colby denied that this conclusion had anything to do with communism or with "any particular social structure which the Russian people themselves may see fit to embrace."

The reason for the American refusal to recognize the Soviet government, Colby said, was that the Bolsheviks, on numerous occasions, had declared that their government rested on the idea that communism must spread to other nations, including the United States. As a result, Colby concluded, "we cannot recognize, hold official relations with, or give friendly reception to the agents of a government which is determined and bound to conspire against our institutions."

Colby's statement froze American and Soviet relations for more than a decade, until normalization took place in 1933 during the first administration of Franklin Roosevelt. Some trade and commerce was revived between the two countries, and a few American citizens traveled to Russia to see the results of the Revolution.

But at the official level there was no contact or dialogue. The one exception in this period came between 1921 and 1923 when Herbert Hoover, then a private citizen, helped to organize a privately funded effort to ease famine in Russia. The American Relief Administration, as it was called, saved several millions of people from starvation and, according to some observers, saved the Soviet government from failure and collapse.

For the past sixty years, Soviet and American relations have followed the pattern established during these early years. The suspicions of Soviet goals expressed by Colby are still the fears of most Americans; Soviet propaganda still attacks the West and the United States and speaks of the eventual victory of communism. The normalization of relations between the two countries in 1933 did not bring an end to their hostility; it merely raised it to an official level. The few attempts at good-will, like Hoover's work during the famine, were quickly forgotten and superseded by renewed resentments and enmities.

CHAPTER TWO
THE COLD WAR

*The main element of any United States policy
toward the Soviet Union must be that of
a long-term patient but firm and vigilant
containment of Russian expansive tendencies.*

George F. Kennan, 1947

The high point in Soviet-American relations was World War II. The war created an "era of good feeling" between the two countries by giving them a common enemy to defeat. The United States sent enormous amounts of supplies and war matériel to the Soviet Union, and the American people learned to admire the courage and perseverance of the Russians, whose suffering in the war was great. Soviet leaders toned down anti-American and anticapitalist propaganda considerably. Many Americans began to hope that an Allied victory over Germany would bring genuine peace and that Soviet and American cooperation might continue in the postwar years.

The new era of peace and cooperation, however, was not to be. Even before the war came to a close, in mid-1945, the relationship had begun to sour, and by early 1946, the Soviet Union and the United States were exchanging bitter accusations. The two nations had emerged from World War II as the dominant world powers, but each had grown deeply suspicious of the other's military strength and of how the other intended to use that strength.

The United States now had the atomic bomb, but the Soviet Union had the largest army on land—an army that had occupied most of eastern Europe and the eastern sector of the defeated German nation. Many Americans had died in the war, but the United States remained unscarred by wartime devastation. America was ready for peace and hopeful that the revitalization of its economy caused by the war would continue.

The Soviet Union, on the other hand, had experienced widespread destruction. The large Soviet army had been maintained only at great expense to the Russian nation. Russia, too, was ready for peace, but it was equally eager to consolidate its wartime gains and to rebuild its economy and society.

On February 9, 1946, Stalin made a speech in the Kremlin on the postwar intentions of the Soviet Union. The USSR, he said, would have to make tremendous exertions and sacrifices in order to recover its strength and vitality. But in confident and forceful tones, he predicted that the destruction brought by the war would soon be overcome and that the Soviet Union would become more powerful than ever before. "Only then," he concluded, "will our country be safeguarded against all eventualities." Stalin reasserted the Marxist-Leninist notion that war between the capitalist countries was inevitable as they competed for markets, but made no mention of the inevitability of war between the Soviet Union and the West.

Stalin may have meant the speech to be primarily defensive in tone, an effort to revive the spirits of war-weary Russians and to give his people a sense of security. Many Americans, however, regarded it with fear and suspicion. Associate Justice of the Supreme Court William O. Douglas, a liberal, called the speech a "declaration of World War III." And for James Forrestal, secretary of the navy, it was proof that democracy and communism could not live together and that a peaceful solution to the Soviet-American rivalry was impossible.

On March 5, 1946, a month after Stalin spoke in the Kremlin, Winston Churchill gave his views on the developing confrontation between the East and West. "From Stettin in the Baltic to Triest in the Adriatic," Churchill said, "an iron curtain has descended across the Continent." He also said:

> *Behind that line lie all the capitals of the ancient states of central and eastern Europe. Warsaw, Berlin, Prague, Vienna, Budapest, Belgrade, Bucharest and Sofia, all these famous cities and the populations around them lie in the Soviet sphere and all are subject in one form or another, not only to Soviet influence but to a very high and increasing measure of control from Moscow.*

Churchill did not believe that the Soviet Union wanted war, but the Russians, he claimed, did want "the fruits of war and the indefinite expansion of their power and doctrines." The only answer to this threat was military power and vigilance, for there was nothing, Churchill said, that the Soviets "admire so much as strength, and there is nothing for which they have less respect than for military weakness." To oppose the Soviet challenge, the former prime minister of Great Britain suggested that the United Nations offered the best hope. But he warned that the UN alone would be ineffective unless there developed a "fraternal association of the English-speaking peoples."

Churchill's speech was not well received by the American State Department which considered it unduly warlike. Several prominent senators and citizens, like Eleanor Roosevelt, the widow of the late President, publicly dissociated themselves from its implications. But Churchill had delivered his speech at Fulton, Missouri, at the invitation of President Truman who shared the speaker's platform with the British leader, and Churchill's words were regarded in many quarters as what the American government privately believed.

In the Soviet Union, the speech was widely attacked and denounced. Stalin accused Churchill of "unleashing a new war" with dire consequences for mankind. The Soviet leader likewise took umbrage at Churchill's call for an English-speaking association and declared the idea to be a "race theory" which claimed that only the "English-speaking nations are full fledged nations . . . called upon to decide the fortune of the entire world."

REINFORCING THE IRON CURTAIN

Between 1945 and 1947, according to Zbigniew Brzezinski, an expert on Soviet affairs and adviser to Presidents Johnson and Carter, the United States and the Soviet Union jockeyed for a superior position in the cold war. The American possession of the atomic bomb and the vastly superior American economy gave the United States the clear advantage in any protracted conflict, a fact that made Soviet leaders very uneasy. But in Europe, which was exhausted by the war and experiencing unsettled social and political conditions, the Soviet army had the upper hand.

What followed, Brzezinski argues, was a period of Soviet "assertiveness" in which the Soviet Union moved in the direction outlined by Stalin in the speech quoted above.* Soviet leaders maintained their large army and did not reduce its size significantly, while the American armed forces had undergone rapid demobilization shortly after the war. Moreover, the Soviet army remained firmly in place in the regions it had conquered in eastern and central Europe.

Elsewhere in Europe, Communist activity was on the increase. Movements led by local Communist leaders established new regimes in Yugoslavia and Albania. In Greece and Turkey, Communist insurgents threatened to unseat governments friendly to the West. The large Communist parties of France and Italy were taking advantage of postwar chaos and uncertainty to increase their power and influence.

By 1948, Soviet intentions in eastern Europe had become clear. In February of that year, a pro-Soviet *coup d'état* in Czechoslovakia established a Communist government in power and eliminated all political opposition. In Poland, Hungary, Romania, Bulgaria, and East Germany, Soviet control was tightened and increased. And in 1949, a long civil war in

---

* One group of American historians, called the "revisionists," place most, if not all, of the blame for the cold war on the shoulders of the American government. Another group of historians hotly protests this position. This author, like many of the young historians in the Soviet Academy of Science, prefers not to place the blame on either side, but looks upon the cold war as the result of a series of misunderstandings, suspicions, and rivalries that soon got out of hand and developed into full-blown hostility.

China came to an end with the success of the Chinese Communists, who had strong support from Moscow.

Other examples of Soviet behavior and Communist activity likewise alarmed the West. In the new United Nations and in other organizations of international collaboration, Soviet officials were disruptive, greedy, and hostile. Soviet leaders seemed reluctant to come to any agreement with the United States on efforts to restore political and economic stability to Europe. Nor did they provide any meaningful cooperation on the settlement of problems raised at the war's end, such as what to do with the defeated German nation.

During this period, too, the American public was distressed by a renewed "Stalinization" of Soviet society and life. The idealistic days of Soviet-American cooperation in the war had led many Americans to expect a "liberalization" of the Soviet government once the war had been won. But by 1946, new stories of Soviet tyranny and rigidity began to spread, along with rumors of trials and purges and other attacks on Soviet citizens displeasing to the government. Stories and rumors of Soviet ruthlessness in eastern Europe shocked the people of the United States and western Europe.

THE POLICY OF CONTAINMENT

To many American leaders, it seemed obvious that the different facets of Soviet behavior formed a pattern. Some believed this pattern was a "master plan" for world domination, a plan drawn up in Moscow and followed methodically to bring communism to every nation. Others discounted the notion of a master plan and argued that Soviet behavior was primarily opportunistic. Soviet leaders, they claimed, would take advantage of situations in order to promote the security and improve the position of the USSR.

American leaders, however, were in agreement that Soviet behavior had to be curtailed. To meet the Soviet challenge, the Truman administration developed what came to be known as "a policy of containment." The policy took form over several months, but was first articulated publicly in an article by George Kennan in *Foreign Affairs* in 1947.

"The main element," Kennan wrote, in the American attitude toward the Soviet Union must be "a long-term patient but firm and vigilant containment of Russian expansive tendencies." It was within the power of the United States, he added, "to increase enormously the strains under which Soviet policy must operate" and "to force upon the Kremlin a far greater degree of moderation and circumspection." In this way, America can "promote tendencies which must eventually find their outlet in either the breakup or the gradual mellowing of Soviet policy."

The policy of containment worked on two levels, economic and military. In order to rebuild Europe and restore political and social stability, the United States instituted the Marshall Plan, a program of massive economic aid and assistance. Named for General George Marshall, the secretary of state, the plan poured enormous sums of money into Great Britain, France, Germany, Italy, and other countries. Marshall Plan monies were also offered to the nations of eastern Europe, including the Soviet Union, but were rejected by Stalin because of fear of undue American influence.

The Marshall Plan was largely successful. Communism lost its attractiveness to many people as their countries were restored to prewar levels of economic and social well-being. But the economic assistance of the Marshall Plan alone was not enough. The policy of containment included the Truman Doctrine, which emphasized the need for American military aid to countries facing Communist-led insurgency.

In March 1947 President Truman laid down in a message to Congress the basic principles of the doctrine that was later to take his name. "One of the primary objectives of the foreign policy of the United States," Truman declared, "is the creation of conditions in which we and other nations will be able to work out a way of life free from coercion."

The United States, the President continued, will not be able to realize its own objectives "unless we are willing to help free peoples to maintain their institutions" in the face of aggressive movements that threaten to establish totalitarian governments. "I believe," he concluded, "that it must be the policy of the United States to support free peoples who are resisting attempted subjugation by armed minorities or by outside pressure." Truman's concern was directed primarily toward the Communist-led guerrilla movements in Greece and Turkey, but his doctrine was one that could be expanded to meet Communist aggression anywhere in the world.

The policy of containment led the United States to encourage greater unity among American allies in Europe. In March 1948 five western European nations—Great Britain, France, the Netherlands, Belgium, and Luxembourg—signed the Treaty of Brussels. This treaty was the first specific Western alliance against a Russian attack and established permanent organizations for joint military action in case any of the signatory nations were invaded.

The next year, 1949, the Brussels Treaty was expanded. Now called the North Atlantic Treaty Organization, or NATO, the member nations, in addition to the five mentioned above, would eventually include the United States, Canada, Iceland, Italy, Norway, Denmark, Portugal, Greece, Turkey, and West Germany. By 1950, NATO had a combined force of fewer than three million men under arms, compared to the Soviet Union's more than four million, but the Western alliance was nevertheless an impressive display of unity and strength.

THE BERLIN BLOCKADE

The first major cold war confrontation between the Soviet Union and the United States came in 1948. Known as the Berlin Crisis, it involved one of the thorniest problems of postwar diplomacy: the future status of the defeated German nation and its former capital, Berlin. Both Germany and Berlin had been divided into four sectors after World War II, governed by the French, British, Soviets, and Americans. The Western powers hoped that the four sectors would eventually be joined into an economic whole, a new Germany whose military power would be severely limited so that it would never again pose a threat to world peace.

It soon became evident, however, that the Soviet Union refused to relinquish its sector, now known as East Germany. Moscow controlled its sector with an iron hand, and looked upon it as conquered territory. Much of the machinery, industrial equipment, and other matériel that had survived the war was removed from the country in payment for the damage Germany had inflicted on the Soviet Union. East Germany was rapidly becoming a Soviet satellite.

Early in 1948, the United States, Great Britain, and France acted on their own to improve the economic situation of their sectors of Germany. Reforms were instituted that led to an immediate stimulation of the economy and to an improvement in living conditions for many Germans in the Western sectors. The Soviets became alarmed that these reforms would be regarded with envy by the East Germans and that Soviet authority in the sector would be undermined.

Soviet leaders believed they had one means at hand to challenge the West: Berlin. Berlin lay well within the borders of East Germany. The main highways and railroads to the city ran through East German territory and could be shut off at a moment's notice. If Western access to Berlin were stopped, then the American, British, and French sectors of the city would collapse and German confidence in the security provided by the Western powers would be shattered.

On June 24, 1948, the Soviets instituted a land blockade, preventing travel to Berlin from the West by road, canal, and rail. The action could have been interpreted as an act of war, but the West did not place this interpretation on it. Instead, the Americans and the British instituted an airlift, called "Operation Vittles." This massive airlift—at its height more than eight thousand tons of matériel were being flown daily into the city—supplied the food, fuel, clothing, and raw materials that the Western sectors of Berlin needed to survive. By May 1949 the Soviets admitted defeat and withdrew the blockade. By a means short of war, the Western nations had faced up to a serious Soviet challenge and had overcome it.

THE KOREAN WAR

The next major cold war confrontation came in Korea. Like Germany, Korea was a divided country. In the northern section of the country, the Democratic People's Republic of Korea had been established with Soviet help and support. In the South, the Republic of Korea, under American influence, had developed its own government and institutions.

In June 1950, the army of Communist North Korea invaded the South. It was assumed in the West that the invasion had the approval of the Soviet Union and was therefore another example of Soviet expansionism. The United States acted quickly through the United Nations to "contain" the new aggression. The UN Security Council, at American urging, condemned the invasion and demanded the immediate withdrawal of North Korean troops behind the 38th parallel, the border that by international agreement separated North and South Korea. When the demand was ignored, the United States sent troops to aid the South Koreans, acting under the banner of the United Nations.

By October 1950, the North Koreans had been driven back near the Chinese border. Troops from Communist China now joined the North Koreans, while other United Nations troops joined the Americans. The cold war had become a "hot" or fighting war, endangering world peace and stability. But the Korean War did not develop into World War III. The Soviet Union did not send ground troops to support the North Koreans, although it did send arms, war matériel, and fighter pilots. Nor did the United States or the Soviet Union, which had recently exploded its first nuclear bomb, resort to atomic warfare. The vital interests of neither country were involved in Korea to the extent that warranted all-out action. The Korean War became a stalemate and was settled finally in 1953 with the partitioning of the country at the 38th parallel, as it had been before the war.

At the beginning of the Korean War, anti-Communist hysteria in the United States came to a head. The hysteria had been mounting for some time. American concern for Communist expansion abroad turned inward, causing many people to suspect Communist subversion in the United States. The House Un-American Activities Committee investigated radicals and leftists of all stripes. One person who was investigated by the committee was a former high State Department official, Alger Hiss. He was eventually convicted of perjury in a case in which he was accused of collaborating with the Russians and holding strong Communist sympathies.

The anti-Communist hysteria found its chief exponent in Senator Joseph McCarthy, a Republican from Wisconsin. In a speech delivered at Wheeling, West Virginia, in 1950, McCarthy declared that he had documented information that showed there were many Communists at work in the State Department. The speech sent a shock wave through the nation and made McCarthy famous overnight. And over the next three years, McCarthy continued to make accusations of Communist activity and subversion throughout the government.

None of McCarthy's accusations were ever proved. Nevertheless, many career public officials lost their jobs when they fell under suspicion. McCarthy bitterly attacked the policies of President Truman and his administration which, he said, were not sufficiently anti-Communist. He later called into question the integrity of Protestant clergymen, elements of the American armed forces, and President Eisenhower himself. McCarthy was eventually condemned by the Senate for his behavior, but he had revealed the depths of fear and hostility that communism could arouse in the American public.

During the early years of the cold war, the pattern of the rivalry between the Soviet Union and the United States became clear. Obsessed with its own insecurity and economic weakness, the Soviet Union began a program of massive rearmament and reindustrialization to turn itself into a superpower threatened by none. Fearful of Soviet ambitions, the United States began to rebuild and expand its military machine to confront the dangers of Communist expansion.

Communist "assertiveness" was met by an American "policy of containment." The Soviet Union remained in firm control of eastern Europe, but was stopped in its bid for Berlin. And communism, too, was prevented from expanding into South Korea. The Marshall Plan and the Truman Doctrine had helped bring peace and stability to Europe and to shore up pro-American governments in Turkey and Greece. But the Soviet-American relationship still remained highly volatile and no one knew where it would lead. The inability of either power to come to an understanding with the other boded ill for the future, as did the large and increasing number of nuclear weapons and other modern armaments possessed by both.

CHAPTER THREE
THREE ATTEMPTS
AT DÉTENTE

Our epoch, the main content of which is
the transition from capitalism to socialism
begun by the Great October Revolution, is
. . . an epoch . . . of the triumph of socialism
and communism on a world scale.

Pravda,
December 6, 1960

Let every nation know, whether it wishes us
well or ill, that we shall pay any price,
bear any burden, meet any hardship, support
any friend, oppose any foe to assure the
survival and the success of liberty.

From the Inaugural Address
of President John Kennedy
January 20, 1961

In the early 1950s, the relationship between the Soviet Union and the United States was at a low point. War raged in Korea between Communist and Western troops, and Europe was divided into two antagonistic blocs, one dominated by the Soviet Union and the other friendly to the United States. In 1953, however, two events occurred that prepared the way for change. In January, a new administration under President Dwight Eisenhower took office in Washington, D.C., and in March, the leader of the Soviet Union, Joseph Stalin, died in the Kremlin. Of the two, Stalin's death was to have the far greater impact on Soviet-American affairs because it made possible the appearance of new Soviet leaders with new ideas about international affairs.

Within six months of taking office, the Eisenhower administration negotiated an end to the Korean War. At the same time, it began to strengthen the United States and to achieve a military superiority over the Soviet Union that could not be challenged. The foreign policy of the new administration was largely formed by the secretary of state, John Foster Dulles, who was deeply anti-Soviet.

Richard Barnet, an expert on international politics, has called Dulles "probably the purest ideologue in power on either side in the U.S.–Soviet confrontation." Dulles believed in the moral superiority of the United States and in America's special responsibility to undermine the Soviet Union's drive for power and respectability. The concepts associated with his name are "massive retaliation" and "brinkmanship."

Massive retaliation, or deterrence, meant that the American nuclear arsenal and the combined strength of its armed forces would be so enormous that any enemy would be profoundly reluctant to launch an attack, since America's reply would mean widespread destruction of the enemy's war-making capabilities. After 1953, the United States undertook a crash nuclear weapons program that emphasized production of bombs and the ability to deploy them in bases in Europe. By 1955, when the Soviet Union had only 350 bombers capable of delivering nuclear bombs to targets in America, the United States had more than four times as many planes capable of delivering such bombs to targets in the Soviet Union.*

Brinkmanship was a word coined by Dulles' critics to describe his policies. It came from an interview with Dulles published in *Life* magazine in 1956. "You have to take chances

---

* During this period, both superpowers also acquired the hydrogen bomb, a far more devastating device than the atomic bomb. The Soviet Union tested its first H-bomb a few months before the United States tested its own.

for peace," Dulles said, "just as you must take chances in war."
He continued:

> *The ability to get to the verge of war without getting*
> *into the war is the necessary art. If you cannot mas-*
> *ter it, you inevitably get into wars. If you try to run*
> *away from it, if you are scared to go to the brink,*
> *you are lost.*

Going to the brink, then, meant being prepared for dangerous
confrontation where American interests were involved, but at
the same time maintaining control of events so that war did
not result. It was a difficult game to play, but it reflected
Dulles' concern that communism be controlled and curtailed.

Under Dulles, the State Department expanded America's
commitments abroad in an effort to establish throughout the
world a system of defensive alliances against communism.
NATO had been the first such alliance. Now it was joined by
the Southeast Asia Treaty Organization (SEATO) and the
Central Treaty Organization (CENTO). SEATO was an
agreement among the United States, Great Britain, France,
Australia, New Zealand, Pakistan, Thailand, and the Philip-
pines, and was primarily directed against Communist China.
CENTO was an agreement among Turkey, Pakistan, Iran,
Great Britain, and the United States against Soviet penetra-
tion of the Middle East.

This period also saw the expanded use of the Central Intelligence Agency (CIA), which had been established in 1947
and was under the direction of Allen Dulles, the brother of
the secretary of state. In Iran, CIA operatives helped overthrow a government friendly to the Soviet Union and return
the pro-American Shah to power. In Guatemala, the CIA was
successful in unseating a leftist regime and replacing it with a
government tied to American interests. The CIA was active in
other parts of the world as well, as was its Soviet counterpart,
the KGB.

THE GENEVA SUMMIT TALKS

Just as the Eisenhower administration put its own stamp on
U.S. foreign affairs, the change in Soviet leadership, following

Stalin's death, brought a shift in that country's policies. By 1954, the international climate had changed. The new Soviet premier, Georgi Malenkov, made gestures that were regarded as friendly by the West. He announced in a speech delivered in the Kremlin, that the Soviet Union stands, as it has always stood, "for the peaceful coexistence of the two systems." A nuclear war, he added, would cause universal destruction—a result that would be beneficial to no one.

On July 18, 1954, a summit conference was convened in Geneva, Switzerland. Attending were President Eisenhower representing the United States, Soviet representative N. A. Bulganin, and representatives of Great Britain, France, and other countries. Eisenhower opened the conference on a note of goodwill. "The American people," he declared, "want to be friends with the Soviet peoples." He went on to say:

> *There are no natural differences between our peoples or our nations. There are no territorial or commercial rivalries. Historically our two countries have always been at peace. . . . It is time that all curtains whether of guns or laws or regulations should begin to come down.*

Eisenhower proposed broad new approaches to the outstanding problems between the United States and the Soviet Union, including the problems of German reunification, free communication between East and West, and peaceful uses of atomic energy. But his most striking proposals concerned disarmament. He called for the Soviet Union and the United States to "give each other a complete blueprint of our military establishments" and to "provide within our countries facilities for aerial photography . . . where you can make all the pictures you choose and take them to your own country to study." These steps, Eisenhower concluded, would prove to the world that the two superpowers were taking measures designed to prevent surprise attacks, thereby "lessening danger and relaxing tension."

For his part, Bulganin proposed a prohibition on the manufacture of nuclear weapons and a limitation of the Soviet and American armies to 1.5 million each. The conference, however, soon bogged down in specifics. The Soviets rejected the American proposals totally, and when it came to their own, they refused to allow on-site inspection, which made any agreement on nuclear arms manufacture meaningless.

This first, tentative move toward détente thus ended in failure. The representatives had gone to the Geneva Conference speaking of a new spirit of cooperation and understanding—often called the "Spirit of Geneva"—but they left with no visible improvement in Soviet and Western relations. Part of the problem was Soviet recalcitrance and distrust of Western motives; part of the problem, too, was the recalcitrance of Americans like Dulles, who remained deeply antipathetic to communism and to Communist leaders. At one point in the conference, Dulles turned his back on a Chinese delegate, Chou En-lai, rather than shake hands with him.

Soviet experts like Zbigniew Brzezinski believe that the United States might have made more of the "Soviet interest in détente" in this period. The Soviet desire to come to a new understanding with the United States in the years immediately following Stalin's death, Brzezinski argues, revealed a "surfacing Soviet weakness" that could have been exploited to America's advantage. But the moment passed and the Soviet-American relationship remained unchanged.

THE HUNGARIAN REVOLT

In February 1956 the "thaw" in Soviet society and politics following Stalin's death reached its climax. Nikita Khrushchev, first secretary of the Soviet Communist party, denounced Stalin in a long, rambling speech that lasted for several hours. The occasion was the Twentieth Party Congress, an event that brought Communist leaders from around the world to Moscow.

The former dictator, Khrushchev said, had ruled Russia with a "cult of personality." He had centered all authority in himself and had not turned to the party leaders for advice and counsel. This, Khrushchev implied, was a violation of Marxist-Leninist principles. Furthermore, Stalin had ruled brutally, had made mistakes in both foreign and domestic affairs, and had done much that was detrimental to the Soviet Union.

Khrushchev's speech was made at a secret session of the Party Congress, but before long, news of its contents was leaked to the world and the effect was electric. In the nations of eastern Europe, hopes ran high that the Stalinist-type governments would be dismantled and replaced by more liberal regimes. By the fall of 1956, changes were coming about. In Warsaw and Budapest, the capitals of Poland and Hungary, reform was in the air, and efforts were being made to relieve these countries of tyranny and dictatorship.

The developments in Poland remained peaceful; those in Hungary did not. During the summer, the Soviets had removed the hated Stalinist boss of Hungary, Mátyás Rákosi, from power but had replaced him with an almost equally despised man. The Hungarians wanted more than this. On October 23, a demonstration was held in Budapest in favor of Imre Nagy, a former prime minister. By the next day, the situation had broken out in civil war. Demands for change came from all elements of Hungarian society, the army, workers, students, and the people of the small towns and countryside.

After several initial skirmishes with the Hungarian people, the Soviet army of occupation withdrew. Imre Nagy became the new prime minister, and the establishment of a moderate Communist government was announced, along with an official declaration of neutrality—which meant that Hungary was severing its connection with the Soviet Union.

The Soviet Union, of course, regarded these events with deep misgivings. Successful reforms in Hungary were likely to be met with demands from other eastern European peoples for similar reforms. The result would be a decrease in Soviet influence and the loss of the buffer states that separated Russia from the West. On November 4, the Soviet army once again began to put down the rebellion. The Hungarians attempted resistance, but were rapidly and brutally defeated by the vast superiority of the Soviet troops.

The invasion and the harsh repression that followed were loudly denounced in the West. To many, Khrushchev seemed to be little different from Stalin in his ruthlessness and use of power. When the smoke cleared and the bitterness aroused by the invasion disappeared, two facts were apparent. First, the

Soviet Union planned to remain in control of eastern Europe and was ready to take any measures to maintain its authority there. Second, for all his talk about the curtailment and control of communism, John Foster Dulles had done nothing to aid the Hungarian rebels or support them in their drive against the Soviet Union. To Khrushchev, this was proof that there were definite limits on the steps the United States was willing to take in the cold war and that Dulles' talk of going to the brink had been just talk.

KHRUSHCHEV AND THE U.S.

In the fall of 1957, less than a year after the Hungarian invasion, the Soviet Union launched the first unmanned satellite into orbit around the earth. Nikita Khrushchev and other Soviet leaders took great pride in the achievement. To them Sputnik I, as the satellite was called, was proof that Soviet science and technology had pulled abreast of science and technology in the United States. There followed a period of Soviet assertiveness in the Soviet-American relationship that Zbigniew Brzezinski has called the era of "premature Soviet globalism"— premature because the Soviet Union did not yet have the military and economic power to play the predominant role in world affairs it wanted to play.

During this period, Khrushchev boasted that the Soviet Union and communism would overtake the United States and the nations of western Europe in every field of human endeavor. He publicly claimed that Soviet factories were turning out hundreds of hydrogen bombs and warned the United States, "I have told Americans: 'you have missiles that can send up oranges. We have missiles that can send up tons. Imagine the kind of bombs that could be contained in our missiles compared with . . . yours.' "

Unlike his predecessors in the early post-Stalin days, he claimed to have little fear of war. Indeed, Khrushchev declared, a war could have its "progressive" aspects. "As a result of World War I," he explained, "Soviet Russia became a socialist country. As a result of World War II, twelve other countries became socialist countries. As a result of World War III, should it ever be launched by the imperialists, capitalism will be eliminated."

But Khrushchev's character was complex. Much of his talk was boast and swagger, and he could be brutal, arrogant, and crude. No doubt his sinister speeches and warnings were meant to shock. But even at his most boastful and arrogant, many political analysts agree, Khrushchev was well aware of the dangers of nuclear warfare and wanted to come to a genuine accommodation with the United States. He wanted, however, to arrive at this accommodation from a position of power, rather than from a position of weakness, and that was one reason for his boasting.

Moreover, writes John Lukacs, the foremost historian of the cold war, new "developments were becoming evident" by 1958 that were altering the Soviet-American relationship. "It was evident," he writes, "that the American and the Russian leaders were no longer crediting each other with immediate warlike intentions" in spite of what was being said on both sides. Not even the "most extravagant Communists," Lukacs claims, "wished to consider the prospects of a hydrogen war." Precisely because of the existence of these horrible weapons, he concludes, "it was becoming evident to both sides that . . . some mutual accommodations in a shrinking world could not be avoided."

From the time he came to power, Khrushchev wanted to visit the United States and had tried to get himself invited on several occasions. In many ways, he admired America and had stepped up Soviet and American exchanges in several fields—science, theater, athletics, commerce, and the investigation of the Antarctic. In the summer of 1959, a Russian exhibition opened in New York and an American exhibition opened in Moscow. Each of these events seemed to imply that a new Soviet-American relationship was at hand.

Vice-President Richard Nixon flew to Moscow to open the American exhibition, and it was there that final plans were made for Khrushchev's visit to the United States in the fall. By any standards, Khrushchev's visit was extraordinary. It was the first tour of the United States by a major Soviet leader. He and his wife visited large cities and small towns. They were taken to large factories and to an impressive farm in Iowa.

The climax of the visit was to be a meeting with President Eisenhower at the presidential retreat at Camp David, Maryland. Khrushchev later wrote that he feared at the time that the meeting had been scheduled at Camp David as a slight to the Soviet Union. "I was suspicious. . . . I couldn't for the life of me find out what this Camp David was. . . . Our foreign ministry didn't know what it was either." When Khrushchev discovered that Camp David was a favorite spot of Eisenhower's and in no way a slight to the USSR, he admitted feeling "ashamed" by his suspicions. "It shows how ignorant we were in some respects," he added.

The meeting, however, resulted in no substantive gains. Afterward, the Soviet press talked of the "Spirit of Camp David" in the same tones used to discuss the "Spirit of Geneva" five years earlier. But like the Geneva Conference, the Camp David summit's achievements were largely illusory. The two leaders agreed on a vague moratorium on the "Berlin question," which left the basic issues involved unsolved. They also agreed to hold a second summit conference the following year, and Eisenhower was invited to make a state visit to the Soviet Union.

Camp David, however, was regarded as the possible beginning of a new understanding—a détente—that might lead to a permanent settlement of the problems of Berlin, nuclear weapons, and disarmament. But once again, everything went wrong. On May 5, 1960, only two weeks before the summit conference was to meet in Paris, Khrushchev angrily announced in Moscow that an American plane had been brought down in the heart of the Soviet Union. The Soviet leader went on to say that the Russians had the plane, which was later identified as a U-2 reconnaissance plane, and that its pilot was in their custody. Furthermore, the pilot, a young American named Francis Gary Powers, admitted that he was employed by the CIA and had been engaged in aerial photographic espionage.

The U-2 incident was clearly a violation of international law and was exploited by Khrushchev for the benefit of the

Soviet Union. From the beginning, the situation was handled badly by Washington. President Eisenhower first claimed that the plane had lost its way in Russian territory while studying the weather and that it was not a spy plane. A few days later, he admitted that the Russian story was correct and that the plane was indeed on an espionage mission. The President at first announced that he had ordered the U-2 flights discontinued, then denied he had made the order, and then confirmed that he had made it.

In harsh, brutal language, Khrushchev denounced the United States. He called off the Paris summit meeting and broke up a ten-nation disarmament conference that was being held in Geneva. In Russia, and throughout the world, the trial of Francis Gary Powers for espionage was given wide publicity and used as a means to berate the United States. The second period of détente—which Soviet expert George Kennan regards as having offered the best chance for improved Soviet-American relations since the 1920s—came to nought, the victim of zealous American espionage and Soviet self-righteous anger.

TIMES OF CRISIS

The U-2 incident and the cancellation of the summit meeting brought a new chill to the cold war. In 1957, Mao Tse-tung, the Chinese Communist leader, had declared that "the East wind prevails over the West wind." Now, Soviet leaders behaved as though history had swung to their side. In a speech of January 6, 1961, Khrushchev noted that for several years, "the initiative in the international arena has been in the hands of the Soviet Union." The capitalist "states and their governments," he added, "defend themselves with their backs to the wall" while the prestige and "foreign political stock" of the West and the United States "have never been so low."

During this period of Soviet initiative, Khrushchev promised support for "wars of liberation" in Asia, Africa, and South America—anywhere guerrilla bands and other leftist movements struggled against Western influence and "American imperialism." Aid and support were given to the Sukarno regime in Indonesia and to the revolutionary government of Fidel Castro in Cuba, which had come to power in 1959. Khrushchev also applied pressure on the West to reach some accord on the Berlin question, promising that the Soviet Union would take matters into its own hands if something were not done.

The armaments race was speeded up. Khrushchev cut the number of Soviet ground troops, but added significantly to his country's missile force and to its stockpile of nuclear weapons. Both the Soviet Union and the United States were spending about $40 billion a year on defense, an enormous sum in those days.* American defense planning was moving in several directions at once. The number of missiles in the American arsenal was increased to match the Soviet increase. And counter-insurgency forces were strengthened to counter Soviet support for wars of liberation. The idea, as stated by the Department of Defense, was to create an American armed force that would enable the United States to fight at least "two and a half wars" simultaneously, should the need occur.

President Eisenhower left office in January 1961. His Farewell Address to the nation was gloomy. Progress toward peace and freedom, he said, "is persistently threatened by the conflict now engulfing the world. It commands our whole attenton, absorbs our very beings." The United States faces "a hostile ideology—global in scope, atheistic in character, ruthless in purpose, and insidious in method. The danger it poses promises to be of indefinite duration."

The new President was John Kennedy, a Democrat from Massachusetts. Kennedy was totally untried in foreign affairs, but he was youthful, intelligent, and as events proved, capable of learning in office. His first experiences in Soviet-American relations, however, were disastrous.

During its last months in office, the Eisenhower administration had begun to make plans for an invasion of Cuba to overthrow Castro. Kennedy inherited these plans and ordered them to continue. In April 1961, three months after he took office, the invasion took place. A force of Cuban exiles, armed and supervised by the CIA, landed in Cuba at the Bay of Pigs.

The invasion, however, had been badly planned and

---

* Because of Soviet secretiveness, defense experts must rely on rough estimates on Soviet spending. Published Soviet figures on their budget are totally unreliable.

badly executed. President Kennedy refused to commit the American air force, and the invading troops were quickly put down by Castro's forces. The result was acute embarrassment for Washington. Once again, the United States found itself loudly denounced by the Communist world as an aggressor and violator of international law.

In June, three months after the Bay of Pigs fiasco, Kennedy met with Khrushchev in Vienna. From the beginning, the meeting went wrong. The Soviet leader used the occasion to browbeat and humiliate the American President and made demands on Berlin and on other problems that he knew Kennedy could not agree to. Vienna, like the Bay of Pigs, ended in complete failure.

The next year and a half found Khrushchev at his most aggressive. On August 13, 1961, the Soviets began to construct a concrete and barbed wire wall to separate their sector of Berlin from the Western sectors. Khrushchev ordered the wall constructed in order to stop the flow of East Germans fleeing to the West, but it was in direct violation of prior East-West agreements allowing free access to all parts of the divided city. About the same time, the Soviet Union resumed testing nuclear weapons in the atmosphere, a move Khrushchev had told Kennedy at Vienna that the Soviets had no plans to undertake.

The Soviet leader's most notable act of aggression began in the summer of 1962. In July and August, Russian ships began to land in Cuba, loaded with fighter planes, Soviet technicians, and missiles. Early in September, the Soviet government warned the United States that any military action against Cuba would result in nuclear war. The Kennedy administration largely ignored the warning, but began to take very close notice of what was happening in Cuba.

On October 14, a U-2 flight over the island brought back photographs of the construction of new missile sites. New photographs made on the following day showed that the sites were rapidly being built and would be capable of delivering missiles in the near future. There were short-range missile sites, with missiles that would endanger the American southeast, and medium-range missile sites, endangering most of the United States.

On October 22, after long and careful discussions with

his advisers, congressional leaders, and representatives of the Organization of American States (OAS), Kennedy went on television with the photographic evidence of the missile sites. He announced that the United States could not accept this "deliberately provocative and unjustified change in the status quo."

The announcement was followed by several days of extreme tension. The U.S. navy surrounded Cuba; American planes patrolled Cuban shores. Twelve thousand marines were placed in readiness and America's nuclear bombers and ICBMs (intercontinental ballistic missiles) were prepared for action. The United States was readying itself for an all-out attack on Cuba and for a nuclear war with the Soviet Union that might ensue.

But then Khrushchev backed down. In late October, he offered to remove the missiles from Cuba if President Kennedy, in return, would promise not to invade the island. Kennedy accepted. Soviet ships in the mid-Atlantic on their way to Cuba were ordered back to Russia. In a few months, the missile sites had been dismantled.

The Soviet Union and the United States had stood on the verge of war, but the war had not come. During the next year, a softening of tension and a new understanding began to develop—the third period of détente. It resulted in the signing on August 5, 1963, in Moscow, of a Test Ban Treaty by the United States, Great Britain, and the Soviet Union, severely limiting the testing of nuclear weapons. The treaty, according to historian John Lukacs, "was a milestone." It indicated that the United States and the Soviet Union had undertaken a revision of cold war rhetoric and a reversal of cold war priorities. And it showed, Lukacs concludes, that "the Peaceful Coexistence of the Soviet Union and the American democracy was no longer merely a disagreeable fact." With the treaty in hand, peaceful coexistence "was an accomplishment of certain standards, an achievement, the crystallization of mature efforts toward a more permanent peace and a more stable world." The Test Ban Treaty was the first tangible result of three attempts at détente. More might have been accomplished, but by 1964 President Kennedy was dead, killed by an assassin's bullet in Dallas, and Khrushchev had been deposed in the Soviet Union.

CHAPTER FOUR
TOWARD A NEW DÉTENTE

Across the gulfs and barriers that now
divide us, we must remember that there
are no permanent enemies. Hostility today
is a fact, but it is not a ruling law.
The supreme reality of our time is our
indivisibility as children of God and
our common vulnerability on this planet.

President John Kennedy

In a speech delivered before the graduating class of American University on June 10, 1963, six months before his assassination, John Kennedy talked about what he called "the most important topic on earth: world peace." A genuine and lasting peace, he said, could not be a peace that was "enforced on the world by American weapons of war." The existence of nuclear weapons, he added, had made peace "the necessary rational end of rational men," but men did not always act rationally.

Kennedy recognized that it was useless to think of peace until Soviet leaders adopted a more enlightened attitude toward Soviet-American relations. "I hope they do" improve their attitude, he said, and "I believe we can help them do it." President Kennedy then went on to acknowledge that America too would have to alter its opinions of the Soviet Union if world conditions were to improve. "But I also believe that we must reexamine our own attitude—as individuals and as a Nation—for our attitude is as essential as theirs."

First, Kennedy claimed, Americans must not regard peace as impossible and war as inevitable. "We do not accept that view. Our problems are manmade—therefore they can be solved by man." Moreover, he pointed out, history has shown that enmities between nations do not last forever, because "the tide of time and events will often bring surprising changes in the relations between nations." To live at peace with one another it is not necessary that men learn to love their neighbors, only that they learn to live together in "mutual tolerance."

For our part, Kennedy said, we must not have a "distorted and desperate view of the other side" that looks upon "communication as nothing more than an exchange of threats." Americans must realize that "no government or social system is so evil that its people must be considered as lacking in virtue." After all, the Soviet and American peoples had characteristics in common that could serve as a basis for agreement and cooperation.

Both, for instance, had a genuine abhorrence of war. "No nation in the history of battle," Kennedy declared, ever suffered more than the Soviet Union suffered in the course of the Second World War. And if a new war should come, he added, everything the Soviet Union and the United States have built "would be destroyed in the first twenty-four hours."

Both nations, therefore, had a "mutually deep interest in a just and genuine peace and in halting the arms race." The people of America must remember that "we are not engaged in a debate, seeking to pile up debating points." Rather, the American purpose must be to conduct its relationship with the Soviet Union so that the USSR would come to see that a move toward peace and arms limitation was in its own best interests. "We can seek a relaxation of tensions," Kennedy maintained, "without relaxing our guard."

A move toward peace requires "increased understanding between the Soviets and ourselves . . . increased contact and communication," the President concluded. If the two countries could not bring all their differences and disagreements to an end, then at least they could work to create a world that was safe for diversity. "For, in the final analysis, our most basic common link is that we all inhabit this small planet. We all breathe the same air. We all cherish our children's future. And we are all mortal."

Kennedy's speech was well-received in the Soviet Union. When it appeared in *Pravda,* Soviet citizens clipped it from the newspaper and carried it around with them. For the first time, an American President had publicly acknowledged the profound suffering of the Soviet Union during World War II. For the first time, the leader of the strongest nation on earth seemed to offer genuine hope for a settlement of outstanding differences between the Soviet Union and the United States.

Kennedy's speech had sounded all the themes of the détente that was later to emerge in the seventies and which he hoped to establish during his presidency. It had spoken of the need for communication and contact. It had recognized that the two nations might learn to live together without fear of total war. And it had emphasized the importance of a reduction of tensions and of arms limitation.

But President Kennedy's speech was ten years before its time. World affairs had not reached a point where meaningful détente was possible. The achievement of the Test Ban Treaty was a significant development, but beyond that it seemed impossible to go. And after Kennedy's death and Khrushchev's fall from power, Soviet-American relations returned for a while to a pattern they had followed earlier in the cold war. The need for better understanding, however, still existed and was to play a part in the moves that eventually led to the détente of the seventies.

VIETNAM AND CZECHOSLOVAKIA

According to Zbigniew Brzezinski, the period between 1963 and 1968 witnessed the "cresting of American globalism." During these years, Brzezinski claims, the United States grew more assertive and gained the initiative in the cold war. Political expert Richard Barnet, who served in the Defense Department and then in the State Department in the sixties, agrees. "This was a time," Barnet has written, "of extravagant imperial rhetoric in Washington and extraordinary overconfidence."

Not long after he took office upon the assassination of President Kennedy, President Lyndon Johnson declared, "we are the number one nation and we intend to stay number one." And in 1965, Robert McNamara, the secretary of defense, announced that the Soviets have "lost the qualitative race" in arms and are no longer "seeking to engage us in that contest." It means, he added, that "there is no indication that the Soviets are seeking to develop a strategic nuclear force as large as ours."

In 1964 and 1965, pro-Soviet governments were overthrown in Brazil and Greece with American help, and replaced with governments friendly to the United States. Again in 1965, President Johnson, concerned with rumors of a leftist takeover in the Dominican Republic, sent American marines to impose order and stability in that country. In 1966, American interests were served in Indonesia with the fall of Sukarno and the establishment of a strongly anti-Communist regime.

But "American globalism" was primarily represented by the Vietnam War. The United States had first been drawn into Vietnam in 1954 when the French, the former colonial masters of the country, were defeated by the Vietnamese. At that time, a political settlement divided Vietnam into a northern half governed by the Communists under Ho Chi Minh (a popular national hero) and a southern half with a government friendly to the West.

The settlement never worked well. North Vietnam aided and supported Communist movements in South Vietnam, and the South, under a series of governments, attempted to resist. In the early sixties, President Kennedy sent American military advisers to help the South Vietnamese. But it was President Johnson who vastly expanded the American commitment in the war.

In 1964 and 1965, the number of American troops in Vietnam began to rise. By 1968, there were more than 500,000 and the war was costing the United States many billions of dollars each year. American aerial bombardment of North

Vietnam began in 1965 and coincided with a visit by Soviet Premier Aleksei Kosygin to Hanoi, the North Vietnamese capital. By the war's end, the United States had dropped more bombs on the North than had been dropped in all of World War II.

Started with the hope of containing communism in Vietnam as it had been contained in Korea and elsewhere, the American commitment in Vietnam proved detrimental to American interests. The war severely divided the United States between those who supported the effort and those who believed it a mistake. It likewise proved to be an enormous drain on American manpower and on the American economy. When it ended, in 1973, Vietnam was united under Communist leadership. Many in the United States regarded it as a defeat, a defeat that did not bode well for America's future relations with the Soviet Union.

Throughout the war, Soviet leaders denounced the United States and the American "act of aggression" in Vietnam. Soviet leaders regarded North Vietnam as an ally and supported her with massive military aid and assistance that made it possible for the North Vietnamese to resist the United States and keep the war going. The Soviet Union, however, sent no ground troops to support its ally, an action that would have undoubtedly widened the war considerably and brought on Soviet-American confrontation elsewhere in the world.

As the United States turned its concentration on Vietnam, Russia turned its own interests toward the improvement of its military establishment. In 1965, Defense Secretary McNamara estimated that the United States had three or four times the number of missiles and bombers possessed by the Soviet Union. By 1968, this superiority in missiles was largely gone, and the cold war advantage so confidently claimed by McNamara three years earlier had disappeared.

The Soviet Union, however, faced problems of its own in this period. In 1968, a reform movement appeared in Czechoslovakia, a Soviet satellite in eastern Europe. A moderate Communist government under Czech leader Alexander Dubcek had come to power. Dubcek promised changes that would make life in Czechoslovakia more comfortable and less rigid. The world press dubbed his movement "communism with a human face."

Once again, as in Hungary in 1956, Soviet leaders believed that a liberal regime in Czechoslovakia would mean a regime no longer tied to the Soviet Union. Along with troops from other eastern European nations, Soviet troops occupied the country and replaced Dubcek with Czech leaders of proven loyalty to the USSR. Compared with the invasion of Hungary twelve years earlier, however, the Czechoslovak invasion was relatively mild. Few lives were lost and little damage was done. But like the Hungarian invasion, the events in Czechoslovakia were regarded in the West as proof that the Soviet Union was still ruthless and dangerous.

CURRENTS OF CHANGE

An observer of Soviet-American relations in 1968 might well have concluded that there was little cause for optimism. The Americans were deeply involved in Vietnam; the Soviet Union had just invaded Czechoslovakia. The cold war seemed "business as usual." A closer look at what Soviet writers like to call the "objective conditions" of world affairs, however, would have revealed new currents and trends which suggested that change might be imminent.

One of these trends was the growing American perception that the United States could no longer serve as "the policeman of the world." Henry Kissinger, who was soon to become national security adviser in the first administration of Richard Nixon, recognized this in 1968. "The United States," Kissinger wrote, "is no longer in a position to operate programs globally." In the future, he continued, the American undertaking "should not be the sole or principal effort" to contain Communism, "but it should make the difference between success and failure." Kissinger recommended that the United States now be concerned with the overall "framework of order" rather than with "the management of every regional enterprise." The various areas of the world, he concluded, must learn to maintain peace and stability in their own regions—with American support, but without the deep American involvement of earlier years.

Kissinger based his recommendations on his perception that during the sixties, the United States had lost the will and determination to carry on the cold war at the level at which it had been maintained for more than two decades. The Vietnam War and the policies of "American globalism" had divided the country as it rarely had been divided before. In its effort to expand its military and political power worldwide, America had discovered the limitations of its power.

Kissinger recognized that in a democracy like the United States, where government policy must bear some relation to public opinion, the will and determination of the people are essential to the government. Without public support, a democratic government loses its authority and must change course. It cannot rely on tyranny or propaganda to induce support where there is none. His recommendations were an effort to bring public policy back in line with public sentiment.

Kissinger also realized that the Vietnam War had brought about a collapse of the nation's foreign policy consensus. Since World War II, Americans had been nearly unanimous in their agreement that Soviet power was an evil that had to be tamed. A large segment of the American public, however, had now come to the conclusion that the image of a world divided into two camps, free and enslaved, East and West, good and evil, had to be discarded.

"The American mood," Kissinger noted in 1968, "oscillates dangerously between being ashamed of power and expecting too much of it." Earlier, American leaders had maintained that America's presence throughout the world was largely the result of American benevolence and goodwill. The United States, they claimed, was a large nation helping small and weak nations to preserve their freedom and independence. But by the Vietnam era, this vision of America had changed. Many Americans now regarded their country not as benevolent and warmhearted, but as a clumsy and narrow-minded giant, enforcing its own will and interests on others and spreading destruction in the process. Americans no longer seemed convinced of the utter rightness of their country's cold war behavior and actions.

The second significant trend or change in the "objective conditions" of world affairs was the growing split between the Soviet Union and Communist China. The split, which first became evident in 1959 and soon widened, was inevitable. The two large Communist nations had deep differences that even their common adherence to Marxism could not disguise. First, the two countries shared a border that ran for more than three thousand miles; historically, it has almost always been impossible for two large, ambitious, and adjacent powers to maintain friendly relations. Second, it was unavoidable that the two chief Communist nations would vie with each other for the dominant position in the Communist movement.

At first, many American observers doubted the authenticity of the split. Some believed that the division between Russia and China was only superficial and that the two would come together in times of crisis. Others doubted that a genuine split existed at all. These people felt that the Sino-Soviet quarrel was a ruse created by the Communists to lead the West into thinking that Communist power was divided and diminished, when it wasn't.

Most experts, however, soon came to the conclusion that the dispute was real. By the mid-sixties, China and the Soviet Union were exchanging verbal attacks that were frequently more stinging than the propaganda either nation leveled against the United States. By the late sixties, their relationship had degenerated even further. Border skirmishes broke out between Chinese and Soviet troops, and both nations amassed large numbers of troops on their frontiers to prepare for possible invasion.

Richard Nixon, who was at the time running for the presidency, emphasized the importance of the Sino-Soviet split in a 1968 article in *Foreign Affairs*. "The deepest international conflict in the world today," Nixon wrote, "is not between the U.S. and the Soviet Union, but between the Soviet Union and Communist China." This conflict, Nixon said, meant that a new era in Soviet and American relations was at hand, if the United States chose to exploit it.

Soviet leaders now faced hostile nations at both ends "of their huge country," Nixon added. In the West, they faced western Europe and the forces of NATO; in the East, they faced China with its billion people. In order to lessen the tensions and dangers created by this situation, he concluded, the Soviet Union must attempt to improve its relationship with the West and the United States. A new Soviet-American understanding would arise out of the Soviet need to deal with the threat of China.

A third "objective condition" that changed in the sixties was economic. The long period of vast American economic superiority was coming to an end. The economic vitality of Japan and western Europe had been restored and was challenging that of the United States. By 1969, the value of the dollar on the world market was beginning to decline. The tremendous costs of the Vietnam War were taking their toll, and there was a growing belief among American economists that the United States could no longer afford to maintain its commitment to a worldwide containment of communism.

NEW LEADERSHIP;
NEW POLICIES

Each of the trends mentioned above—the decline of America's will and determination, the decline of its economy, the collapse of its foreign policy consensus, the split between China and the Soviet Union—was making its influence felt in the world of the late 1960s. Each contributed to the détente that began in the next decade. But the events that helped to precipitate that détente and to hasten its arrival were first, a new presidential administration under Richard Nixon in Washington and second, the development of new approaches to international problems by the leaders of the Soviet Union.

Richard Nixon was uniquely placed to improve Soviet-American relations. His chief interest as President was foreign affairs, and his reading and experience in that field were broad. But most importantly, he had the reputation of being a strong anti-Communist. As a young member of Congress, he had risen to fame on the basis of his attacks on Communist activity at home and abroad; the most important piece of legislation he had sponsored was the Mundt-Nixon Bill that dealt with subversion in the United States. As Vice-President and later as a private citizen, he continued to defend America and to denounce Soviet expansion and behavior. No one, then, could attack Nixon for being "soft on Communism" or for looking at Soviet-American relations unrealistically.

Even before taking office, Nixon and his national security adviser, Henry Kissinger, had come to the conclusion that the Soviet Union should no longer be regarded as a "revolutionary" power, but rather as a "legitimate" member of the family of nations. This did not mean that American and Soviet differences could be reconciled or forgotten; it did mean that Soviet-American relations could be placed on a new level of understanding. For many years, Soviet leaders had attempted to gain recognition as a legitimate power, and a move by the United States in this area would open up a new field for discussion and perhaps cooperation between the two countries.

Kissinger believed that the Soviet Union had first proved itself to be a legitimate, responsible nation at the time of the Cuban Missile Crisis. At that time, Khrushchev and the Soviet leadership had come to a realization of what nuclear war would mean for the world and had backed down, rather than face confrontation with the United States. The Test Ban Treaty that followed was the first significant step in defusing East-West tensions.

Dr. Kissinger also believed that the Sino-Soviet dispute had helped to legitimize the Soviet Union. The dispute had helped to deter Russia from a purely revolutionary course by breaking the momentum of the world Communist movement. No longer, Kissinger argued, could Soviet leaders be obsessed with spreading communism as they once had been. They now had concerns—chiefly their rival China—that would force them to behave in a more acceptable manner.

Finally, Kissinger believed that American interests would best be served by the establishment of a long-term understanding with the Soviet Union, rather than by reacting to particular crises when they sprang up. He wanted the United States to abandon its "obsession" with what Soviet *intentions* were and turn its attention toward a new Soviet-American relationship. "The obsession with Soviet intentions," Kissinger wrote, "causes the West to be smug during periods of tension and usually evokes purely military counter-measures."

The ultimate goal of Americans in the past, Kissinger said, had been a "change in the Soviet system." But this goal, like the concentration on Soviet intentions, was unrealistic. A more realistic and rational attitude would be one that sought concrete agreements based on interests common to the two powers—without demanding that there be a clear understanding of the intentions behind the agreements or that the Soviet Union change to please American taste.

Thus, the change Kissinger proposed in East-West relations was very basic: the abandonment of twenty-five years of confrontation and the acceptance of the notion—raised by John Kennedy in his American University speech—that in order to deal with the Soviet Union, the United States was going to have to learn to live with it and accept its existence. Kissinger's views were essential to détente. Without what George Kennan has called Kissinger's "imagination, boldness of approach, and sophistication of understanding," détente would have been impossible.

Changes in the perceptions of American leaders were not the only perceptual changes taking place in Soviet-American relations. The thinking of Soviet leaders was also undergoing alteration. This alteration was due partially to a new measure of self-confidence on the part of Soviet leaders. The Vietnam War had given them a picture of American vulnerability and the limitations of American power. After 1968, as American power began to decline and Soviet military power increased, this measure of self-confidence increased.

But the most significant change on the part of Soviet leaders came with their perception of the needs of Soviet society and the measures that had to be taken to answer these needs. The 1962 Cuban Missile Crisis had given the Soviet Union a vision of its own weakness from which it did not easily recover. What followed was a renewed effort to meet the American challenge and surpass it.

This goal, however, proved elusive. By the late sixties, it

had become apparent that the Soviet hope to match American per capita production in the near future was impossible. The U.S. still produced twenty-five times as many cars as the Soviet Union and four times as many trucks. Soviet agriculture was still only one-sixth as productive as American agriculture. The rate of increase in Soviet industrial production was in decline. Soviet industry was growing at a slower rate than it had in the 1950s, and the industries most seriously affected by this stagnation were those most essential to the modernization of the Soviet economy: the production of consumer goods, petrochemicals, computers, and electronics.

In Stalin's time, these deficiencies would have been covered over, disguised, or concealed. Khrushchev would have met them with bluster and boasting. But a new set of leaders now governed the Soviet Union, and these leaders approached government in a new way. Russian expert Wolfgang Leonhard has described this new leadership, which included at the top Leonid Brezhnev and Aleksei Kosygin, as "more realistic, more objective, and more oriented to the present" than any Soviet leadership in the past.

The new leadership recognized that a great many of the Soviet Union's problems were tied to the giant Soviet bureaucracy and its inability to create and carry out meaningful improvements. In 1965, Premier Kosygin had emphasized this point in a speech to other party leaders. "In the course of analyzing many important problems," he said, "we often find ourselves prisoners of laws we ourselves have made, which should have been replaced long ago by new principles corresponding to the modern conditions that govern the development of production."

State planning, Kosygin said, "is not only an economic activity, as people often believe. It is the solving of social problems linked with the raising of people's standard of living." In order to improve the Soviet economy and society, he concluded, "we have to free ourselves completely . . . from everything that used to tie down the planning officials and obliged them to draft plans otherwise than in accordance with the interests of the economy."

This new, innovative attitude on economic matters spilled

over into the Soviet attitude toward the West. The new leaders of the Soviet Union realized that if economic life in Russia were to improve, they would have to turn to the West for technological and industrial assistance. And economic and technological agreements with the West would only be possible if East-West relations were established on a new basis. In this way, Soviet economic backwardness helped pave the way for détente.

DÉTENTE IN WESTERN EUROPE

In its move for improved relations with the West, the USSR first established détente with two of America's principal allies in Western Europe: France and West Germany. Détente with the Soviet Union had long been one of the goals of the great French leader Charles de Gaulle. De Gaulle's initial attempt to improve relations with the USSR had come in 1944, before the end of World War II. At that time, he proposed a French-Soviet alliance to reflect earlier alliances between the two nations made in 1892 and in 1935. His aim was the creation of a strong France in postwar Europe, a France that could act as the major mediator between the Soviet Union and what he called "the Anglo-Saxon camps"—the United States and Great Britain.

De Gaulle's proposal to Stalin fell on deaf ears. Twenty years later, however, the French leader, who was once again in power, renewed his proposal. The new steps toward détente began in 1965, when Soviet Foreign Minister Andrei Gromyko visited Paris. Gromyko's visit was followed a few months later by the visit of de Gaulle's foreign minister, Maurice Couve de Murville, to the Soviet Union.

In Moscow, Couve de Murville was told by Premier Kosygin that the Soviet Union was deeply concerned about America's involvement in the Vietnam War. Since the USSR was supplying arms to America's enemy, North Vietnam, Kosygin said that the Soviets regarded themselves as at war with the United States. The French government decided nevertheless to proceed with détente, in spite of the Soviet indication of a bad relationship with France's ally, the United States.

Early in 1966, France announced that it was withdrawing from NATO and asked for the removal of all American and foreign military installations. In June, de Gaulle made a triumphant tour of the Soviet Union where he met Communist party Secretary-General Leonid Brezhnev. De Gaulle's ultimate program for French-Soviet relations was "détente, entente, and cooperation." He hoped for an eventual understanding between his country and the USSR that would allow the two nations to dominate Europe "from the Atlantic to the Urals." The understanding would exclude Great Britain and the United States, whose influence in European affairs de Gaulle wanted to bring to an end.

The Franco-Soviet détente was met in the United States with great misgivings. American leaders believed that the French withdrawal from NATO weakened the Western alliance and thereby strengthened the Soviet Union. American critics of de Gaulle also pointed out that the Franco-Soviet détente was an agreement between vastly unequal "partners" where the French gave much and gained little, while the Soviet Union gave little and gained much. The French leader, however, remained firmly behind his move.

West Germany approached détente with the Soviet Union from completely different motives. Since World War II, West German policy had been based on the eventual reunification of the two Germanys, the eventual unification of Europe, and upon a strong relationship with the United States. Since Soviet policy was specifically opposed to each of these programs, there seemed to be little basis upon which a relationship between the Soviet Union and West Germany could be built.

The French withdrawal from NATO, however, and the Franco-Soviet détente shook West German policy to the core. Coupled with these developments was the involvement of the United States—upon whom West Germany deeply relied—in the Vietnam War. Many West German leaders came to the conclusion that it was time to establish German foreign policy on a new basis, and that new basis, by necessity, included a new relationship with Russia.

The first steps were taken in 1969 when a moderate leftist regime came to power in Bonn under Chancellor Willy

Brandt. In August, a Soviet-German Treaty was signed, followed by a Polish-German Treaty in November. The two treaties accepted what German policy had so long denied. The border between East and West Germany was accepted as official, and the two Germanys were declared to be "two German states in one nation." This formula recognized the division of Germany, but at the same time suggested that the two countries shared a common national past that bound them together in a special way.

What West Germany believed it had received by détente was a recognition of the peculiar position West Germany occupied between East and West. "Our national interest does not permit us to stand between the East and the West," Chancellor Brandt explained in 1970. "Our country needs cooperation and harmonization with the West and understanding from the East." West Germany had lost nothing in the new arrangement with the Soviet Union, he maintained, which had not already been "gambled away" long ago. What détente had proved, he concluded, was that West Germany had had "the courage to open a new page in history."

By the time Brandt uttered these words, the Nixon administration had begun to take tentative steps toward détente and was opening its own "new page in history." It is now time to look at the contents of that détente and analyze the new Soviet-American relationship that emerged in the seventies.

CHAPTER FIVE
DÉTENTE ACHIEVED

We do not bring back from Moscow the promise
of instant peace; but we do bring the beginning
of a process that can lead to a lasting peace.

Richard Nixon
in his July 1, 1972, message to Congress
on his visit to the Soviet Union

"For the first time in a generation," President Nixon told the
nation in a radio message on February 9, 1972, "we have
taken a series of steps that could mean a new relationship with
the Soviet Union." These accomplishments, he said, had not
come about by accident. They were the result of careful planning and the work of a government willing to adopt new ideas
and practices in order to meet new problems. "Three years
ago," Nixon went on, "we stopped reacting on the basis of
yesterday's habits and started acting to deal with the realities
of today and the opportunities of tomorrow."

Indeed, the Nixon administration had accomplished
much in a short amount of time and had moved ahead on
several fronts. It had begun a new series of talks with the Soviet
Union on arms limitation and had reached an accord with
Russia on the Berlin question. Through careful preparation, it
had established contact between the United States and Communist China. And it had begun to lay the basic framework

for détente. Events moved fast during Nixon's first administration; most Americans were still thinking in the cold war terms of an earlier period as the new Soviet-American relationship rapidly took form.

The Berlin accord and the opening of contact with China were among the first of these developments to bear fruit, and they helped make the others possible. Berlin was at the top of Nixon's foreign policy priorities. He regarded it as the chief stumbling block in Soviet-American relations and believed that if détente were to prove to be possible, Berlin would have to be the first question resolved by the two powers. When West Germany reached its own détente and settlement with the Soviet Union in 1970, the stage was set for Soviet and American negotiations.

A "quadripartite agreement" on Berlin was signed on June 3, 1971, by representatives from the United States, the Soviet Union, France, and Great Britain. The first section of the agreement declared that "the four Governments will strive to promote the elimination of tension and the prevention of complications in the relevant area." Further stipulations required that the Soviet Union would not impede travel between West Germany and Berlin, that steps would be taken to improve communications between West Berlin and the areas of East Germany adjacent to it, and that West Berlin would not be governed from West Germany.

The accord contained several advantages for both sides. It gave American approval to the settlement already reached by West Germany and the Soviet Union. It helped to lessen tension between the USSR and the United States by removing the thorniest part of the Berlin problem—access to West Berlin—from debate.

As a result of the agreement, travel to West Berlin became freer. The city, once isolated and alone, now seemed more open and accessible. Telephone communications between West Berlin and East Germany were restored.* And

---

* Prior to the accord, telephone calls from one section of the city to the other had to be routed through Copenhagen and Moscow. After the accord, an inhabitant of West Berlin could call a friend in East Berlin directly, and vice versa.

several thousand East Germans were able to take advantage of provisions in the new accord to emigrate to West Germany. As the American secretary of state, William Rogers, said when the protocol on the agreement was signed: "For the people of Berlin the agreement offers an improvement in daily life. Once only the stark effects of division could be seen in Berlin. Now the start of a healing process is in sight."

Nixon regarded the Berlin accord as a turning point because it proved the willingness of the Soviets to undertake serious negotiations and arrive at meaningful conclusions. The next step was a summit meeting in Moscow which the Soviet and American leaders scheduled for May 1972. Meanwhile, the president turned his eyes toward China.

The opening of contact with Communist China was perhaps the most striking event in this period of extraordinary developments. As President Nixon later admitted, "twenty-five years of hostility stood in the way" of Chinese-American friendship and made negotiations between the two countries "painstaking and necessarily discreet." Henry Kissinger prepared the way for the new relationship on a secret mission to Peking in 1971. The following year, Nixon made the first visit by an American leader to mainland China.

Nixon looked upon his visit to China as the beginning of a "process of communication" that promised much for the futures of both countries. Both the President and leading members of his administration were careful to deny that the cultivation of friendship with China was directed against the Soviet Union. But most political observers believed otherwise. The American courtship of China, they said, was obviously done to put pressure on the Soviet Union to improve its own relationship with the United States. Why else, they asked, had Nixon made his move toward China, unless it was to compel the Russians to meet the threat of Chinese and American cooperation?

THE PRINCIPLES OF DÉTENTE

Nixon's visit to China came in February 1972; the trip to Moscow was to be in May. In the months before the summit, the President made it clear that he hoped to gain "substance" from the meeting, not mere "atmospherics." Earlier summit meetings—Geneva and Camp David—had resulted in vague improvements, called "the Spirit of Geneva" and "the Spirit of Camp David," that had lasted a short time and disappeared. This was atmospherics. Nixon wanted, instead, agreements that would last and new attitudes that would endure.

From the President's point of view, the Moscow summit was a success. He and Mrs. Nixon and the American entourage, which included Secretary of State Rogers and Henry Kissinger, toured three major Soviet cities: Leningrad, Kiev, and Moscow. On May 29, at the conclusion of the visit, Nixon and Soviet leader Brezhnev signed a "Text of Basic Principles" which outlined the various aspects détente was to take. The President invited Secretary-General Brezhnev and other Soviet leaders to visit the United States "at a mutually convenient time." The Soviet leaders accepted the invitation.

The "Text of Basic Principles" had a long subtitle: "Basic Principles of Relations Between the United States of America and the Union of Soviet Socialist Republics." After a short introduction, the Text listed twelve principles that were to govern Soviet and American relations in the future. These principles, Kissinger later said, served as a "road map" for détente and offered a code of behavior by which each nation could judge the other.

The first principle stated that the two superpowers would "proceed from the common determination that in the nuclear age there is no alternative to conducting their mutual relations on the basis of peaceful coexistence." Differences in ideology, it concluded, "are not obstacles to the bilateral development of normal relations based on the principles of sovereignty, equality, non-interference in internal affairs and mutual advantage." A relationship based on these principles implied that the United States had fully accepted the Soviet Union as a legitimate power in international affairs.

Principle Two said that the U.S. and the USSR "attach major importance to preventing the development of situations capable of causing a dangerous exacerbation of their relations." To avoid these situations, the two nations promised to do their utmost to avoid military confrontations and nuclear war by exercising restraint in their relations. They also agreed to conduct future negotiations in the spirit of "reciprocity, mutual accommodation and mutual benefit." The use or threat of force was renounced, and both nations agreed that efforts "to obtain unilateral advantage at the expense of the other" were inconsistent with peace and stability.

The remaining principles required the Soviet Union and the United States "to do everything in their power" to prevent the rise of tensions anywhere in the world and "to promote general peace and security." They welcomed an increase of contact between American political leaders and Soviet leaders and stated a firm belief in the importance of increased commercial and economic ties between the Soviet Union and the United States. And they deemed it "timely and useful" to develop mutual contacts in the fields of technology and science and to deepen ties between the two nations by promoting "improved conditions for cultural exchanges and tourism."

Principle Eleven was particularly interesting and significant. It stated that "the U.S.A. and the U.S.S.R. make no claim for themselves and would not recognize the claims of anyone else to any special rights or advantages in world affairs. They recognize the sovereign equality of all states." Henry Kissinger interpreted this agreement as a renunciation of "any claim to special spheres of influence" anywhere in the world.

In his message to Congress upon his return from Moscow, President Nixon said that "an unparalleled opportunity has been placed in America's hands. Never has there been a time when hope was more justified or when complacency was more dangerous." He continued:

> *We have made a good beginning. And because we have begun, history now lays upon us a special obligation to see it through. We can seize this moment or we can lose it; we can make good this opportunity to build a new structure of peace in the world, or let it slip away.*

Indeed, the twelve principles did offer a "new foundation" for Soviet-American relations, if the two nations lived up to them. The President's obvious pride in his achievement was justified.

But Nixon's foreign policy was not without its critics, and in time these critics would grow more vociferous. The principles, they said, were too general and vague and gave the advantage to the Soviet Union.

THE SALT TREATY

The strategic arms limitation talks—known as SALT—were the most complex part of détente and the most important because they dealt with the arms race. The complexity of the negotiations was due to the sophistication of modern weapons systems—some of which can be understood only by experts—and to the nature of the arms race. How, for instance, was the United States to verify that the Soviet Union was sticking by any agreement that was made on arms limitation? How was either nation to spot evasion or dishonesty when whole strategic and defensive weapons systems were involved in the discussions? And how were the two antagonistic powers to come to an agreement that was equitable and which offered each country a reliable means to maintain its national security?

President Nixon began planning for arms talks with the Soviet Union as early as the spring of 1969. At that time, he appointed a group of senior governmental officials, called the Verification Panel, to be responsible for planning and conducting the American side of the SALT negotiations. Henry Kissinger was to act as chairman of the panel and was to be assisted by an under secretary of state, the deputy secretary of defense, the chairman of the Joint Chiefs of Staff, the director of the CIA, and the director of the Arms Control and Disarmament Agency.

The work of the Verification Panel was difficult. It had to analyze, on the basis of the best expertise available, each of the weapons systems that would be involved in the negotiations. All problems had to be looked at in all possible combinations, in order to anticipate any difficulties that might arise. The aim of the panel, Dr. Kissinger said, was to be on top of the issues involved in SALT so that when stalemates developed, alternative solutions would have been analyzed ahead of time and "ready for immediate decision by the President."

Negotiations with the Soviet SALT team began in November 1969. The first major breakthrough was announced on May 20, 1971. The Soviet Union had made an important concession, followed by another from the United States. The USSR agreed to "ignore" what are known as the American "forward-based systems"—the aircraft carriers, submarines, and short-range bombers operating from bases near the Soviet Union, each capable of carrying nuclear weapons to Russia in a short amount of time.* In return, the United States abandoned its request that both powers be limited to an equal number of offensive long-range missiles, thereby granting the Soviet Union a three-to-two edge on ICBMs.

At this time, the SALT teams agreed that their negotiations would take two forms. The first would deal with offensive weapons, the second with defensive weapons. Offensive weapons were those considered capable of being used to launch an attack against the enemy, such as the missiles mentioned in the previous paragraph; defensive weapons, like the ABMs, or antiballistic missiles, were those that could be used to shoot down and destroy an enemy's missiles after they had been launched and before they could cause damage. Since offensive systems were the more complex part of the issue, it was decided that the initial settlement on offensive weapons would be an interim treaty, not a permanent one, and that it would freeze only selected categories of weapons at agreed upon levels. The settlement on defensive weapons, on the other hand, would be permanent.

In its final form, the SALT I Treaty, which went into effect September 25, 1972, allowed the Soviet Union and the United States each to have one ABM site for the defense of its national command authority and another ABM site for the defense of its intercontinental ballistic missiles. The treaty also required that the two ABM defensive systems be at least 800 miles (1,300 km) apart in order to prevent the development of a territorial defense.

---

* Some experts estimate that at least thirty thousand of these nuclear weapons could hit the Soviet Union and that many would strike Russia within six minutes of launching.

Each of the two sites was permitted to have 100 ABM interceptors. Prohibitions were placed on the establishment of radar bases for the defense of populated areas or the conversion of air-defense missiles to antiballistic missiles. Both the Soviet Union and the United States were given the right to withdraw from the Treaty on six month's notice. It should be noted that one reason for these defensive agreements was that neither side wanted the other to perfect an effective system of defense. A nation that possessed an effective system of defense, which would protect its population and military capability from utter destruction, would no longer fear its enemy. It might then feel confident enough to launch an attack on its opponent.

On the offensive side, the Treaty froze the number of missiles in the Soviet and American arsenals at levels currently under operation or under construction. This meant that the United States would have 1,054 ICBMs, the Soviet Union 1,618. At the same time, the Soviet Union agreed to freeze the number of its heavy ICBM launchers and accepted limitations on the number of its submarines and submarine-launched missiles. A prohibition was also placed on the conversion of light ICBMs into heavy missiles, so that neither side could disguise its true number of heavy ICBMs.

Henry Kissinger defended the terms of the Treaty before a congressional committee. "It is clear," he said, "that the agreement will enhance the security of both sides." He emphasized that SALT I was "embedded . . . in the fabric of an emerging relationship"—détente—that had great historical significance. "For the first time," Kissinger pointed out, "two great powers, deeply divided by their divergent values, philosophies, and social systems, have agreed to restrain the very armaments on which their national survival depends." These agreements should be given a chance, he declared, in order to place Soviet-American relations "on a new foundation of restraint, cooperation, and steadily evolving confidence."

The second point Kissinger made before the committee was that SALT I in no way weakened the posture of the United States. The Treaty, he said, "perpetuates nothing which did not already exist in fact and which could only have gotten worse without an agreement." The agreements, he maintained, "fully protect our national security and our vital interests."

Americans, Kissinger went on, must not be dismayed by the fact that the USSR has more weapons than the United States. "The quality of the weapons must also be weighed," he argued, and American warheads were significantly more accurate than Soviet warheads. Moreover, American nuclear technology was superior to Soviet nuclear technology, and with the American MIRVs (multiple, independently targeted re-entry vehicles), the United States has a two-to-one lead in the number of warheads. Overall, Kissinger concluded, the Soviet Union may have a larger number of weapons, but it is the number of weapons "which is limited by the agreement."

Kissinger stressed that President Nixon was "determined that our security and vital interests shall remain fully protected." This could be done, he added, not only by the acceptance of SALT I, but also by pushing "the next phase of the Strategic Arms Limitation Talks with the same energy and conviction that have produced these initial agreements." President Nixon and his national security adviser, therefore, saw SALT I as a beginning to be followed by SALT II and other negotiations leading to further significant reductions in arms.

OTHER IMPORTANT AGREEMENTS

In addition to the Berlin accord, the Moscow summit's twelve principles, and SALT I, the era of détente also produced a series of significant agreements in other fields. The most important of these were in trade and commerce and in science, technology, and cultural exchange—all areas in which Soviet and American contact had existed before but now expanded.

The Nixon administration regarded increased contact in these fields as a means to create a "web of entanglements" between the two countries. This web would foster and multiply communication at all levels and make each country more reliant on the other. The Nixon administration also believed that a "web of entanglements" was essential to détente, for if Soviet-American relations failed to move ahead on all fronts, then any single agreement, like the Berlin accord or SALT I, might lose ground, and the Soviet-American relationship would fall back into old patterns of behavior.

Besides, there were practical and concrete advantages for both sides if agreements could be reached in these fields. We have seen in the last chapter how the Soviet leadership believed it was necessary to turn to the West for help in the improvement of Soviet economic and technological problems. This need was articulated in the published guide for the Five Year Plan of 1976–1980, which called for "wider participation in the international division of labor and raising the role of foreign economic ties in resolving economic tasks" that face the Soviet Union. In short, Soviet leaders desired the scientific and economic expertise they could acquire from the United States and elsewhere.

There were also benefits for the United States. Many observers believed that the large multinational corporations pressed détente because it offered the opportunity to open the Soviet market—a nation of more than 250 million—to investment and expansion. The Soviet Union offered perhaps billions in profits at a time when the American economy had become sluggish, when the country was importing more goods than it was selling abroad. Expanding commerce with the Soviet Union could help reverse this negative balance of trade that the United States was experiencing for the first time in a century. Moreover, the United States could benefit from areas in which Soviet science excelled.

Détente at the level of trade and commerce began in November 1971, when Maurice Stans, the secretary of commerce, handed the Soviet minister of foreign trade, Nikolai S. Patolichev, a "letter of understanding" that listed conditions for increased trade relations. Eleven months of negotiations followed, in which two key problems emerged. The first was the settlement of the debt the Soviet Union owed the U.S. from the lend-lease program of World War II. The second problem arose from the difference between the two country's economic systems. How could the United States, with its market economy, deal with the Soviet Union, where the state controls trade.

The lend-lease problem, according to State Department Assistant Secretary Willis Armstrong, "represented the need to settle a legitimate claim for goods used in the Soviet postwar civilian economy—a claim identical to those which all other allies settled—to clear the books before new transactions were undertaken." The Soviet Union had originally taken the position that matériel acquired in the lend-lease program had been paid for with the blood of Soviet citizens during the war. Now an agreement was reached in which the USSR agreed to pay the United States $722 million in a series of installments through the year 2001. The settlement of this problem opened the way for further agreements in the area of trade and commerce, including the extension of trade credits to the Soviet Union by the United States.

Agreement on the second problem—how the two very different economies were to deal with each other—proved more difficult. Soviet leaders were eager to preserve the economic independence of the Soviet Union and feared that the economic vitality of the United States would prevail in any Soviet-American economic relationship. But in this area, too, compromise was reached, and included the following provisions:

• The Soviet Union and the United States agreed to make available to each other trade credit arrangements "which are usual and customary in the financing of exports."
• The Soviet Union agreed that it would not ship products to the United States which will "cause, threaten, or contribute to the disruption of" the American market.
• The agreement allowed the Soviet Union to place substantial orders for American machinery, plant equipment, agricultural products, and consumer goods, and predicted that the total Soviet-American trade would triple in value within three years. Specifically, the Soviets made known their interest in buying American equipment to manufacture tableware, in acquiring American help to build their huge Kama River truck manufacturing industry, and in several other projects amounting to many millions of dollars.
• The Soviet Union promised to make available business facilities in Russia for American business interests equivalent to those granted trade representatives of other nations. An American trade office was to be established in Moscow and a Russian counterpart in Washington.
• Both the Soviet Union and the United States agreed to encourage third-country-supervised arbitration for any disputes that arose under the new trade agreement.

Under the new Soviet-American trading and commercial relationship, trade did begin to increase between the two countries. In July and August 1972 the Soviet Union bought more than nineteen billion tons of wheat from the United States and was to continue buying more in the following years. Before 1971, American exports to the Soviet Union rarely amounted to more than $100 million a year, but in 1976, four years after the signing of the trade agreement, they reached $2.5 billion.

The breakthroughs in the agreements on science, technology, and cultural exchange came, like the trade agreements, during the first six months of 1972 and were later expanded and revised. These agreements included:

• The establishment of a U.S.–Soviet Joint Commission on Scientific and Technical Cooperation to oversee cooperation in the scientific and technical fields.

• A "joint docking experiment" in space arranged by the U.S. National Aeronautics and Space Administration and the USSR Academy of Sciences. The experiment, which was in the planning stages for several years, took place in 1975. Soviet cosmonauts and American astronauts rendezvoused in space and visited one another's spacecrafts.

• An Agreement for Cooperation in Peaceful Uses of Atomic Energy which gave American scientists access to Soviet large-scale breeder reactor technology in which the United States lagged behind, and gave Soviet scientists access to American expertise in magnetohydrodynamics to build a pilot power project.

• An Agreement on Cooperation in Medical Science and Public Health which was designed to combat the "common enemies, disease and disability." The chief areas of mutual concern were to be heart disease, cancer, and the environment. Scientists and doctors of the two nations began to share laboratory and clinical research and to exchange equipment, information, and biological specimens. Developments in cancer therapy in each country were examined and tested in the other. In 1974, an artificial heart agreement was signed, and collaboration on the development of methods for "total heart replacement" was planned.

• A "Memorandum of Implementation of the Agreement Between the United States and the Union of Soviet Socialist

Republics on Cooperation in the Field of Environmental Protection" that was signed on May 23, 1972. The Memorandum listed eleven areas of common concern beginning with air pollution and including sections on water pollution, pollution related to agricultural production, enhancement of the urban environment, marine pollution, earthquake prediction, and ecology. These problems, said President Nixon in a message to Congress, were "mankind's common problems" and both American and Soviet leaders recognized the responsibility of the wealthier, industrialized nations to find solutions for them.

• An agreement that noted the American awareness of the extensive English language training programs in the USSR and that indicated an American intention to encourage Russian language programs in the United States.

• The decision to step up exchanges of individuals between the Soviet Union and the United States. As a result, hundreds of Russian scientists and scholars visited the United States, and American scientists and scholars visited the USSR. American and Soviet historians began to cooperate on joint archival research. And the exchange of art exhibitions and other forms of artistic endeavor were stepped up.

THE HELSINKI AGREEMENT

On August 1, 1975, the United States and the USSR signed the Final Act of Helsinki. In diplomacy, a "final act" implies an agreement of a political, rather than a legal, nature. Helsinki was the last important achievement of détente and was the result of negotiations by the Conference on Security and Cooperation in Europe. In addition to the U.S. and the Soviet Union, it was signed by thirty-three other nations.

Several parts of the Helsinki agreement amounted to pledges to strengthen and broaden détente. The participating states declared their full support for the United Nations and promised to respect one another's "sovereign equality and individuality." They renounced the "threat or use of force" and subversion in settling international disputes. And they gave particular emphasis to the establishment of "fundamental rights, economic and social progress and well-being for all peoples," as well as to the need to promote world peace.

The nations that signed the Helsinki agreement also recognized the present borders in Europe as inviolable, an acceptance by the United States and the West of the status quo in eastern Europe and the Soviet Union. The agreement also called for increased economic and scientific cooperation among the signing nations. And one section of the Helsinki agreement required that NATO and Soviet pact countries notify one another in advance when maneuvers of more than twenty-five thousand men were to take place.

The most significant areas of the Helsinki agreement, however, were in human rights and the free flow of information. The signers pledged themselves to respect "fundamental freedoms, including the freedom of thought, conscience, religion or belief." They agreed, in addition, to improve the "international movement" of people by providing for the "reunification of families" separated by borders and the enhancement of travel for personal or professional reasons.

Finally, the thirty-five signers agreed to improve the circulation of information in their countries and to arrange for better public access to materials, including books, films, and other media that traveled across national borders. Each nation was required to improve the working conditions of journalists and grant them freedom of movement. And there were to be broader cooperation and more frequent exchanges in the areas of culture and education.

The Helsinki agreement was the final step of the détente that had begun to take root five years earlier. The beginnings of Soviet-American cooperation were now a reality on several levels. A framework for a new relationship had been established. It was hoped that improved communication between the two superpowers would increase mutual understanding, reduce isolation and suspicion, and lessen the chances for war.

The new détente—largely the work of Richard Nixon and Henry Kissinger and their Soviet counterparts—was an impressive achievement. By the time of the signing of the Helsinki agreement, the fourth détente had already lasted longer than any of the three earlier periods of détente. But by the time of Helsinki, too, there were already forces and events at work undermining the new relationship, and critics in both countries who wondered if the détente was desirable at all.

CHAPTER SIX
THE END OF DÉTENTE

From the military standpoint the changing
international reality is that the United States has
been shrinking in terms of its relative power,
while the Soviet Union has been growing.

James Schlesinger
secretary of defense, 1976

From the beginning, critics of détente pointed to two serious
flaws in the new Soviet-American relationship. First, the relationship was too new and untried for anyone to know what it
meant. And second, détente was couched in language so vague
and uncertain that it provided, at best, only a dim and very
general outline for the conduct of international affairs. What
was wrong, these critics argued, was that détente could mean
anything the United States or the Soviet Union wanted it to
mean. It was this lack of certainty and reliability that made the
achievements of détente illusory and dangerous.

Indeed, many observers agreed that the United States and
the Soviet Union each had its own definition of what détente
was and that these definitions, at bottom, were very different
and mutually exclusive. For Americans, détente tended to
mean that the United States was willing to enter into a new
relationship with Russia in order to reduce world tension and
lessen the ideological struggle.

American leaders hoped that American aid to the Soviet Union would result in a "web of entanglements" that would tie the interests of the two nations together to the point where war would be unlikely. And some Americans carried the additional hope that détente would lead to a gradual transformation of the USSR and its "closed" society into something less rigid and more liberal.

Soviet leaders, on the other hand, approached détente from a different angle. For them, détente meant increased cooperation with the United States at many levels, but it did not mean that the USSR would cease its struggle to acquire superiority over capitalism. Brezhnev made this point on many occasions. As early as 1970 the same point was made in an article published in the Soviet journal *Leninism Today*. "Peaceful coexistence," the author wrote, "does not extinguish or cancel out class struggle." Rather, it "is a new form of class struggle" that abandons "war as a means of settling international issues" and plans to carry out that struggle on other fronts and in other ways.

Soviet leaders, too, made clear their belief that détente was possible only because Soviet power was increasing, while that of America was decreasing. This point was emphasized by Georgi Arbatov, the director of the Institute on the United States of the Soviet Academy of Science, in an article written after he had accompanied Brezhnev on a visit to the United States.

The enormous "defensive might" of the Soviet Union, Arbatov claimed, was one of "the major objective changes" in recent history. The other, he added, was the erosion of Western imperialism. Arbatov went on to enumerate the weaknesses of American society that were part of that erosion: "inflation and unemployment, the balance of payments deficit . . . poverty . . . the problem of the black population, the crisis and decay of the big cities, the monstrous crime rate, the decline in morals." These problems, Arbatov implied, had caused the United States to seek peace with the Soviet Union. But, he cautioned his Soviet readers, détente should not lead Russians to believe that the United States had altered its basic policies toward the USSR. It had not and could not, because it was still a capitalist country.

The distinction between the American view of détente and the Soviet view has perhaps best been described by the American expert on international politics, David Watt. The Soviet view on détente, writes Watt, is the "status quo *plus*;" the American view is the "status quo *minus*." The Soviets want the status quo plus a continuation of the class struggle at the international level; the Americans want the status quo minus cold war confrontation. The long-term result of this divergence, Watt warns, could be a "tilt in the geopolitical balance of power"—in favor of the Soviet Union.

Thus, what Watt and other critics of détente found disagreeable about détente was that it was an unequal agreement, with the advantage on the Soviet side. They believed, too, that it was an agreement that offered an immediate and tangible threat to the West. The danger, most critics agreed, was that détente would lull the United States and its allies into a false belief that the Soviet military threat had lessened. This illusory belief, they argued, would tend to reduce the willingness of the democratic countries to maintain the military readiness necessary to genuine peaceful coexistence.

REPRESSION IN THE USSR

Part of the problem was the nature of Soviet society and of Soviet leadership. Even as détente began to take root, American experts on the Soviet Union warned about the attitude they found manifested in the USSR. "Having smarted so long," wrote Marshall Shulman, "under what they felt as the 'arrogance' of American strategic superiority, the Soviet leadership is in a chesty mood, prepared to enjoy the advantages of a rising power position." And, according to George Kennan, "the Soviet regime continues to be inspired by an ideology hostile in principle to the Western nations, from which it dares not depart."

Indeed, Western observers of Russia noticed that at the very moment the Soviet Union began to open itself to new agreements with the West, it also began to tighten and close its own society ever more firmly. Wolfgang Leonhard has traced the course of this development. By 1969, Leonhard claims, Soviet leaders saw that due to their country's sluggish economy, the USSR would continue to fall behind the West in science and technology. Furthermore, poor Soviet economic performance would continue the "frightful shortage" of consumer goods in the Soviet Union and "lead to serious unrest among the populace."

This situation obviously needed remedy, but what? For two years, Leonhard notes, there were secret discussions about economic problems in the Soviet leadership, and then at the Twenty-fourth Party Congress of March 1971 Brezhnev announced the "decisive general line" to be followed to meet these problems: a "peace program" and a moderate foreign policy were to be coupled with harsh repression at home.

The aim, Leonhard concludes, was "obviously to extract the maximum possible benefits in trade and technology from the West, and to increase the suppression of their own people, to limit their freedom and the penetration of ideas from the outside." And Brezhnev was also concerned, Leonhard adds, with silencing critics of his policies in Soviet society, particularly party members who desired more liberal reforms than Brezhnev wanted to grant, and conservative neo-Stalinists, who were opposed to any form of détente.

The new repression took the form of more widespread and better organized attacks on the Soviet dissident community and its leaders. The number of searches, arrests, and trials increased. Many prominent figures were involved, including the novelist Alexander Solzhenitsyn, who was forced to emigrate from Russia, and the nuclear scientist Andrei Sakharov, who now lives in exile from Moscow in an industrial city off limits to Westerners. But many less known figures as well have suffered repression and imprisonment.

These events, critics maintain, underline the problem of détente with the Soviet Union. Can a regime that increases repression at home while it turns the hand of goodwill abroad be trusted to live up to its commitments? Should the United States and the West give their approval to this regime and help to strengthen its activities through economic and scientific cooperation?

In an interview with the *New York Times* in 1973, before his exile, Andrei Sakharov severely warned the West about the dangers of détente. Western cooperation with the Soviet Union, he said, would only enable Soviet leaders to concentrate on accumulating strength. "As a result," he added, "the world would become helpless before this uncontrollable bureaucratic machine" that is the Soviet Union. Sakharov pointed out, too, that an unqualified Western willingness to improve relations with the Soviet Union would "mean cultivating a country where anything that happens may be shielded from outside eyes—a masked country that hides its real face." It is these factors, say the critics of détente, that make détente such a risky business.

DÉTENTE: THE CRITICS' VIEW

When the critics surveyed the achievements of détente point by point, they found little that gave encouragement. There were simply too many questions, they believed, about each of the achievements and too little certainty about the benefits gained by the United States.

SALT I. Henry Kissinger argued that détente lessened the chances of nuclear war. Many critics, however, were reluctant to accept this argument. They pointed out that the Soviet Union and the United States had gone to the brink of nuclear war on several occasions in the cold war, but had not gone over. Nuclear weapons were simply too mutually destructive to be considered as a means to settle international disputes. Hence the SALT I Treaty and its limitations on nuclear weapons represented little advance at all, since both nations had lived without nuclear war for thirty years and there was no reason to believe that they would choose to unleash their nuclear arsenals in the future.

The critics argued, however, that a policy that aimed primarily at the problem of preventing nuclear war was going to leave the world with the threat of conventional war. Indeed, the history of the cold war showed that both the Soviet Union and the United States were willing to engage in limited wars where they believed their self-interest was involved. Thus, a détente aimed at preventing possible nuclear war and not at preventing the more probable conventional war was, as political analyst Theodore Draper has pointed out, a policy that left something to be desired. Such a policy, he warned, may "be the easy way out. The more difficult and more pressing problem may well be the prevention of conventional or non-nuclear wars."

But the critics' most chilling assessment of the dangers of détente was based on estimates of Soviet arms buildup during the mid- to late-1970s. Lord Chalfont, a former journalist and member of the British cabinet, has argued "that nuclear balance, always a fragile and uncertain edifice, is being demolished before our very eyes." The Soviet Union, he has maintained, "is resolved to acquire the capacity in the very near future . . . to deliver an effective nuclear attack and survive the ensuing retaliation."

In the United States, Paul Nitze, a national security expert, agrees with Lord Chalfont. Nitze believes that the Russians are developing a "theoretical war-winning capability," because they are constantly improving the accuracy of their missiles, building larger ones, making an effort in civilian defense to keep down their own casualties in case of nuclear war, and are dispersing and hardening their military plants.* These are chilling facts, he argues, because the United States accepted the Salt I Treaty—which allowed the USSR to have a larger number of missiles than the U.S.—only because it was convinced that American missiles were of better quality and accuracy. If the Soviets have vastly improved the quality of their missiles, he concludes, then the American qualitative edge has been lost and American security is threatened. If this is the case, the critics ask, then what has détente brought us except the lull before an even larger and more dangerous expansion of the cold war?

---

* Experts hotly debate the question of whether (and to what degree) the Soviet Union violated Salt I during the 1970s by its military buildup. Some believe that major violations of the treaty occurred and that the Soviet Union acquired a definite military superiority over the United States in the period. Others believe that the case for Soviet superiority is overstated and the USSR remained, for the most part, within the limits defined by the agreement.

Trade and Commerce. The proponents of détente argued that increased trade and commerce between the Soviet Union and the United States would help to create a situation where war was less likely; the opponents wondered if there was any real connection between trade and improved relations. They pointed to the fact that trade between Russia and Germany reached its high points in 1913 and 1940, just before those two nations were engulfed as antagonists in World War I and World War II. Trading and commercial ties had clearly failed to stop major wars in these cases.

Moreover, the critics believed that American negotiators had shown little determination to gain important concessions from the Soviets for trading benefits the United States granted them. This was disquieting, they argued, because arms control and other important problems should have been intimately linked with trade—a concession in trade from the U.S. tied to a meaningful concession from the USSR on arms control or on other matters of interest to the United States. Otherwise, Soviet leaders could use American resources gained through trade to solve Soviet economic problems, while saving their own resources for the continuing military buildup. The United States would be playing the dangerous—and perhaps fatal—role of helping Russia become economically stable, and stronger than ever militarily.

The critics likewise argued that the so-called trade credits the Soviets were granted by the trade agreements were not traditional trading and commerce at all, but outright aid. The Soviet Union could pay for increased trade only by balancing its large amount of imports with the amount of goods exported from the Soviet Union. The best way to achieve this balance was by increasing the exportation of Soviet raw materials, such as oil and gas.

But the USSR, the critics pointed out, had been unable to achieve this balance in trade. That left it no alternative but to ask for trade credits, which must be guaranteed and perhaps subsidized by government. And since it was a question to be handled by government, the expansion of credit to the Soviet Union was a *political* question, involving the political interests and concerns of the United States. To what extent, the critics asked, was America willing to bargain away its economic advantage for the sake of improved Soviet-American relations?

The political nature of trade and commerce, the critics said, was clearly illustrated by the fate of the Jackson and Vanik amendments to the U.S. trade act with the Soviet Union. In the mid-seventies, Senator Henry Jackson (Democrat, Washington) and Representative Charles Vanik (Democrat, Ohio) sponsored a bill in Congress that tied trade concessions from the United States to Soviet concessions in the area of human rights. "When we talk of free trade," Senator Jackson said, "let us also talk of free people. When we bring down the barriers that keep manufactured goods from Communist countries out, let us also bring down the barriers that keep their people in."

Specifically, the Jackson-Vanik amendments were concerned with the Soviet practice of levying a large tax on university-educated citizens seeking to emigrate—a policy directed against Soviet Jews who wanted to move to Israel. The Nixon administration opposed the amendments, because it believed that trade and human rights should not be linked. Congress, however, thought otherwise and the bill passed both houses.

For the critics of détente, the outcome was predictable. Soviet leaders angrily rejected the amendments, saying that they represented a gross violation by the United States of Soviet internal affairs. The new trading and commercial relationship received a blow from which it never fully recovered. The Soviet Union, the critics argued, had shown that it was unwilling to make meaningful concessions when it came to human rights. And if the United States was unable to obtain these concessions, then there was no reason to proceed with détente.

Science and Technology. Robert Ellsworth, the American representative on the NATO Council, underlined the problem of increased scientific and technical exchanges between the U.S. and the USSR in a 1970 *Department of State Bulletin*. Ellsworth recognized that the Soviet "hunger for access to the science and technology of the West" was a key factor in their drive for the "expansion of . . . scientific and technical relations."

Ellsworth recognized, too, that the United States could exploit this "hunger" to lessen cold war tensions and improve Soviet-American relations. Such a policy might gain limited, short-term results, but in the long run, Ellsworth concluded, it was a dangerous path to follow. It gave the Soviet Union the benefit of American scientific and technical superiority, but the most the United States might extract in return was a promise of Soviet "good behavior"—a promise no one could guarantee.

Ellsworth then told the story of the Duke of Urbino who had committed a "classic blunder" four hundred years ago. The Duke, according to Ellsworth, "possessed by far the most advanced artillery of the sixteenth century." He loaned this artillery to Cesare Borgia "for the alleged purpose of a Borgia attack upon Naples." But instead, "Borgia promptly turned the artillery upon Urbino as he had planned all along." Critics of détente wondered if the United States might be repeating this classic blunder. Would American scientific expertise given the Soviet Union during détente be turned against the United States?

The China Factor. In 1972, Henry Kissinger told Theodore White, the noted journalist, that "what the world needed was a self-regulating mechanism." The key to such a mechanism, Kissinger added, was China. The United States, the Soviet Union, and China, he seemed to imply, were evenly matched and no one power would dare to take on a second without the help of the third. This three-power mechanism would help to regulate world affairs and thwart war by taming the aggressiveness of any one of the three nations. The new friendship between China and the United States would restrain and control Soviet ambitions and arrogance. Détente could proceed because the China factor guaranteed that the Soviets could be brought to heel.

The critics, however, never regarded this "triangular theory" of world affairs as very persuasive. China, they noted, was far from the status of a superpower. Its economy was still weak and backward. Its military power could not be compared to that of the Soviet Union or the United States. The "balance" among the three nations was not even and would not be for some time to come. If détente, in part, rested on the China factor, then, the critics concluded, it was resting on a weak basis.

Soviet leaders may have regarded China as a serious threat to the USSR in the sixties, the critics said, but this was no longer true. A massive Soviet military buildup on the Chinese border in the 1970s had eliminated the Chinese threat. And this buildup, the critics pointed out, had not been made by withdrawing Soviet troops from the western part of the Soviet Union. It had been accomplished by an enormous increase in Soviet troops on all fronts, in order to give the USSR maximum freedom of action in case of crisis. China therefore had far more to fear from the Soviet Union than the Soviet Union had to fear from China.

THE ARAB-ISRAELI WAR, 1973

In the first parts of this chapter, we looked at the reasons the critics believed détente to be an illusory, dangerous, and unrewarding course for American policy to follow. In the following sections, we shall look at events which the critics said were specific violations of the agreements reached by the United States and the Soviet Union. The most significant of these violations were the Arab-Israeli War of 1973, Soviet support for revolutionary movements in Angola and Ethiopia, and the 1979 Soviet invasion of Afghanistan.

The opponents of détente argue that the first major Soviet violation of détente came with the Arab-Israeli War of October 1973, sometimes known as the "Yom Kippur War." The twelve "Basic Principles" signed a year and a half earlier at the Moscow summit had said that the two superpowers "have a special responsibility . . . to do everything in their power so that conflicts or situations will not arise which would serve to increase international tensions." The principles likewise required the two nations to "prevent the development of situations capable of causing a dangerous exacerbation of their relations." If the Soviet Union had lived up to these promises, the critics argued, the Arab-Israeli War would never have taken place.

In the first place, the war was preceded by a massive shipment of arms and equipment from the Soviet Union to Egypt. The Egyptians asked for and received advanced surface-to-air missiles and Soviet crews to man the missiles. They received new planes and other modern weapons. Clearly, the aim of the Soviet Union was to exacerbate the world situation by creating an advantageous position for itself in the Middle East.

On October 1, 1973, President Sadat of Egypt summoned the Soviet ambassador in Cairo and informed him that an attack on Israel would be launched in the near future. The exact date was kept secret for security purposes. Three days later, however, Soviet civilian advisers and their families were evacuated from Egypt. This evacuation came about twenty-four hours before the first intelligence reports reached Israel's defense minister, Moshe Dayan, that Egypt was about to begin an attack.

Critics like Leonard Shapiro and Harvard professor Richard Pipes contend that if the Soviets had been serious in complying with the Moscow summit agreements, they would not have sold new arms and weapons to Egypt and would have done more to prevent the war; they could, for instance, have warned the United States that an Egyptian attack on Israel was imminent. The Soviet Union did none of these things. Kissinger's aides argued that it was unrealistic to expect any of these moves.

But if this were true, the critics asked, then what was the meaning of the Basic Principles? Did the Principles mean what they said or were they merely another document that was hardly worth the paper it was written on?

The opponents of détente also emphasized another disturbing factor about the Arab-Israeli War of 1973. They claimed that both Israel and the United States had taken the Moscow Principles quite seriously, and expected the Soviet Union to live up to them. This overly optimistic assessment of détente had then blinded both nations to the meaning of the buildup of Soviet arms in Egypt. As a result, Israel had been rendered vulnerable to surprise attack.

There was evidence to substantiate these claims, the critics said. American intelligence, for instance, had functioned poorly before the outbreak of the war. When the Soviet advisers and their families began their evacuation two days before the attack, some American intelligence officers interpreted it as proof that a deep misunderstanding had developed between the Egyptians and the Soviets, resulting in the evacuation.

On the day of the attack, October 6, the highest level U.S. intelligence report claimed that an invasion was not imminent, and even after news of an Egyptian military action against Israel was received, it was believed that Israel had launched the attack, not Egypt. Had the spirit of détente, the critics asked, so lowered American vigilance that American intelligence could not see and interpret what was going on before its very eyes? And if American intelligence could blunder so seriously in the Middle East, what was it doing elsewhere in the world?

CONFLICTS IN AFRICA

Nor did détente serve as a framework for the settlement of differences between the Soviet Union and the United States concerning the two African nations of Angola and Ethiopia. Trouble had been brewing in Angola for some time. Still a colony of Portugal in the early 1970s, it was engulfed in a civil war among three factions, each of which wanted to take power once independence had been won.

The Soviet Union and the United States were involved in the civil war. One of the factions, the MPLA (Popular Movement for the Liberation of Angola), received help and support from the Soviet Union. Another, the FNLA (National Front for the Liberation of Angola), received aid from the United States. The third, UNITA (National Union for the Total Independence of Angola), received help from the United States, China, and elsewhere.

By 1975 the American government had grown concerned

that the MPLA would emerge victorious in the struggle and allow the Soviet Union to become "a dominant influence in south-central Africa." National security advisers in the Ford administration recommended that help to Angola's FNLA be stepped up. The United States then secretly sent between $30 million and $50 million worth of military equipment to the FNLA and UNITA.

The Soviet Union, however, was answering this challenge with a far more massive shipment of supplies and aid to the MPLA. By February 1976 more than eleven thousand Cuban combat troops were in Angola along with $300 million in Soviet military equipment. When President Gerald Ford and Secretary of State Kissinger requested that American aid be likewise increased, they were handed a resounding no from Congress, which did not want to commit the United States to another Vietnamlike situation. The support of Cuban troops, which eventually numbered twenty thousand, and the Russian military aid gave the MPLA the edge it needed to win the war, and the Soviet-backed faction took power.

"This type of action will not be tolerated again," Kissinger warned, as he cancelled the meetings of several Soviet and American joint committees that were to consider the next stages of détente. But Kissinger did not cancel a large grain shipment to the Soviet Union, nor did he move to delay or suspend the SALT II talks. He did add, however, that détente would not survive "another Angola."

Brezhnev's response came a short time later. "Détente," he told the Twenty-fifth Soviet Communist Party Congress, "does not in the slightest abolish, and cannot abolish or alter, the laws of the class struggle." No one, he continued, should be fooled into believing "that because of détente Communists will reconcile themselves with capitalist exploitation . . . We make no secret of the fact that we see détente as the way to create more favorable conditions for peaceful socialist and communist construction."

John Marcum, the leading American expert on Angola, has pointed out that neither the United States nor the Soviet Union approached the Angolan problem from the point of view of détente. In spite of the Moscow summit promises of consultation in times of crisis, there was no communication between the United States and the USSR at any stage. America, Marcum emphasizes, did not try preventive diplomacy, but left Moscow "to draw its own conclusions about American intentions." Both the United States and the Soviet Union sent military aid to rival Angolan factions, thereby increasing tension in the area and raising the pitch of superpower rivalry. Not three years after the basic framework of détente had been worked out, Marcum implies, both nations were ignoring its provisions.

A crisis in Ethiopia brought on the next Soviet-American disagreement. In 1977, troops from Somalia invaded Ethiopia to regain control of the Ogaden, a province inhabited by Somalis, which had long been under Ethiopian control. The Soviet Union responded by sending thousands of Cuban troops to Ethiopia, along with military advisers and technicians, jet fighters, and tanks. Zbigniew Brzezinski, national security adviser to President Carter, warned that the new Soviet buildup represented "another Angola," but this time with even greater Soviet involvement.

The Carter administration worried that the conflict would spill back over the border into Somalia and that the war would be widened. At the same time, the administration was divided on what to do about the situation. Secretary of State Cyrus Vance favored quiet diplomacy. Ethiopia was, after all, within its rights, according to international law, in asking for outside help to repel a foreign invasion.

Brzezinski favored a more aggressive approach. He wanted to link American concessions in the ongoing SALT II talks with Soviet concessions in Africa. Publicly, Brzezinski declared that the United States had made "substantial concessions" in the nuclear arms talks and had thereby demonstrated its "political will" to reach an agreement. Now he asked the Soviet Union to demonstrate an equal political desire by helping to bring an end to the Ethiopian-Somali War. "We are not imposing linkages," Brzezinski said, "but linkages may be imposed" if the Soviet Union engages in "unwarranted exploitation of local conflict for larger international purposes."

It was Vance's call for quiet diplomacy, however, that

won out. The secretary of state was able to gain private assurances from the Soviet Union that the Somali border would not be crossed. And a new recommendation from Brzezinski that an American naval task force be sent to the area, to prove to the world that the Soviet Union had backed down, was rejected as unnecessary.

Once again, the critics said, détente had done nothing to lessen world tension. Secretary Vance had achieved his demands through traditional diplomatic means, which could have worked without détente. Once again, they claimed, the Soviet Union had ignored the twelve principles for its own personal gain.

Other observers noted, however, that Brzezinski had done great harm to détente by linking the Somali War with SALT II. When the Soviet Union refused Brzezinski's request for concessions in Africa in return for concessions on nuclear arms, much of the remaining political support for détente in the United States evaporated. Brzezinski had put the Soviet leaders on the line and they had refused to play the game, proving, the critics said, that Soviet goodwill in détente was nonexistent when it came to vital Soviet interests.

THE INVASION OF AFGHANISTAN

The Arab-Israeli War of 1973 had begun an erosion of détente. The conflicts in Angola and Ethiopia had led to further deterioration. But it was the Soviet invasion of Afghanistan that led to the lowest point in Soviet-American relations in more than a decade. For many people throughout the world, the Soviet invasion aroused the spectre of earlier Soviet invasions in Czechoslovakia in 1968 and Hungary in 1956. Ten years of détente seemed to have brought nothing but renewed cold war hostilities.

In 1978, a pro-Soviet government had been installed in Afghanistan under Prime Minister Hafizullah Amin. By the middle of 1979, however, the Soviet Union had become disenchanted with Amin, who, it was believed, could not be trusted to remain loyal to Soviet interests. In September, a clumsy, Soviet-supported attempt to assassinate Amin ended in failure when another high government official, Nur Muhammad Taraki, was killed by mistake. Taraki had been Amin's chief rival in Afghan affairs, and he had similarly enjoyed the support of the Soviet Union.

By late September, American intelligence sources reported that "Soviet military involvement" in Afghanistan might be imminent. An anti-Soviet rebellion had spread across the country, and Soviet leaders feared that Afghanistan might be lost to the Soviet bloc if the rebellion were not contained. American experts, however, weighed the pros and cons of a Soviet invasion and came to the conclusion that the Soviet Union would choose to stay out of Afghanistan. The USSR, the experts decided, would not want to anger other Moslem nations in the Middle East, nor would it want to displease the United States and "tip the balance" against SALT II.

From the American point of view, events in Afghanistan and its neighbors Iran and Pakistan soon escalated into a problem of major proportions. On November 4, an angry mob of nationalist and fundamentalist Moslem Iranians seized the American embassy in Tehran and took its occupants hostage. On November 21, Pakistani mobs attacked and burned the American embassy in Islamabad, and the Carter administration began to talk of a "crescendo of crises" that threatened peace and stability. Since both Iran and Pakistan border on Afghanistan, it was feared that the Soviet Union might exploit the situation for its own purposes in the Middle East.

American intelligence sources continued to report a massive Soviet arms buildup on the Soviet side of the border with Afghanistan. On five separate occasions in December, the American government cautioned the Soviet government that intervention in Afghanistan would "have serious consequences" for the relationship between the Soviet Union and the United States.

On December 24, the invasion began. For three days, the Soviet Union airlifted thousands of troops and tons of equipment into Afghanistan; other airlifts were to follow until the total number of troops was more than 77,000 with 1,330 tanks and support personnel. It was an awesome display of Soviet power and ability to carry on war.

Soviet leaders claimed that the invasion was necessary because help had been requested by Prime Minister Amin. "It is the official Soviet position," a Soviet government statement read, "that all its actions in Afghanistan were fully sanctioned by international law, in response to pleas for aid from a nation endangered by foreign agents." The Soviets, however, quickly seized Prime Minister Amin and his family and executed them for "crimes against the state."

The American reaction to the invasion was to scrap the remaining elements of détente. President Carter removed SALT II from his list of priorities. American grain shipments to the Soviet Union were halted. And the Carter administration announced its intentions to stop scientific and technical cooperation with the Soviet Union and to declare a boycott of the 1980 summer Olympics, which were to be held in Moscow. The Soviet invasion was likewise overwhelmingly condemned by the United Nations.

The invasion renewed cold war feelings in the United States. "The implications of the Soviet invasion," Carter told Congress, "could pose the most serious threat to world peace since the Second World War." He warned the Soviet Union that "an attempt by any outside force to gain control of the Persian Gulf region will be regarded as an assault on the vital interests of the United States of America, and such an assault will be repelled by use of any means necessary, including military force."

The invasion renewed cold war fears that the Soviet Union had a "grand design" of world conquest and that the Soviet threat to world peace and stability had to be met by an increased American commitment to arms buildup and improvement of the American armed forces. With Afghanistan, the era of détente had moved into a new period of hostility and suspicion.

CHAPTER SEVEN
THE COLD WAR RENEWED?

Reference has been made here to 'détente'. . . .
If the word has any significance, we must realize
that it does not today exist as an accurate
description of East-West relations. It remains
an objective to be sought, yet to be achieved.

Ambassador Max Kampelman
co-chairman of the American delegation at
the Madrid Conference on Security and
Cooperation in Europe, December 1980

There can be no doubt that the Soviet-American détente that began in the early seventies during the administration of Richard Nixon has come to an end. That détente was closely tied to President Nixon and to his national security adviser and later secretary of state, Henry Kissinger. When Nixon resigned his office, owing to the Watergate scandal, détente lost one of its chief proponents.

Nixon's successors were men with less diplomatic skill and less commitment to the policies that had made the new relationship with the Soviet Union possible. President Gerald Ford continued to pursue détente, but reluctantly. Ford traveled to Vladivostok in the Soviet Union to meet with Brezhnev, but he was a conservative Republican who maintained deep suspicions of Soviet behavior and intentions. During the presidential campaign of 1976, Ford avoided mention of détente, substituting instead the phrase "peace through strength" to describe his policy toward the Soviet Union.

President Jimmy Carter succeeded Ford in office. From the beginning of his administration, Carter managed to antagonize Soviet leaders. He announced a new American foreign policy with an emphasis on human rights. The policy stressed the moral responsibility of the United States to encourage individual freedom throughout the world. Governments like that of the Soviet Union which appeared to abuse human rights were to be condemned, while those which guaranteed the rights of their citizens were to receive support. Soviet leaders looked upon the human rights policy as high-handed and arrogant, and regarded it as a direct intrusion into the private affairs of the USSR. The Soviet Union, they pointed out, did not tell the United States how to handle its internal problems, and the United States should not tell the Soviet Union how to behave.

In Moscow in March 1977 the first meeting between Soviet leaders and Carter's secretary of state, Cyrus Vance, ended in failure. Vance went to Moscow with a proposal for deep cuts in the level of nuclear weapons in the arsenals of both countries. But his proposals and his method of introducing them deviated widely from the pattern of negotiation that had been followed during the Nixon and Ford administrations. And Soviet leaders, dismayed by this deviation from standard procedure and by Carter's human rights policy,* rejected Vance's proposals. It took the Carter administration the better part of two years to recover from this initial Soviet rebuff.

Thus, in part, détente failed because of change in administrations in Washington and because of the different approaches Nixon, Ford, and Carter had in foreign affairs. But these were not the only reasons for failure. As the critics had maintained from the beginning, détente was too new and untried to be trusted fully by either country; the two rivals did

---

* President Carter made no secret of his admiration for the Soviet dissident movement and at one point wrote a letter of support to Andrei Sakharov, the Russian physicist who has been highly critical of the Soviet government and of détente.

not have time to shed the engrained habits and attitudes of twenty-five years of cold war. Each superpower found it easier to deal with the other on the basis of past behavior than to move, without reservation, into the new relationship promised by détente.

The feelings of superiority and inferiority that have plagued Soviet-American relations from the beginning also played their part in the failure of détente. Each nation felt comfortable in dealing with the other only from a superior position; fears of inferiority aroused distrust and misunderstanding. The Soviet Union began a massive rearmament program not long after it had experienced humiliation at the time of the Cuban Missile Crisis of 1962. The United States turned its attention toward improvement of its armed forces after its confrontation with military inferiority in the mid- and late-1970s. In both cases, the result was a renewed arms race and renewed world instability.

Détente has now degenerated into a series of charges and counter-charges. The Soviet Union accuses the United States of violating Soviet-American agreements by improving its relationship with China and by strengthening its forces in NATO. Both developments, the Soviets say, upset international equilibrium and increase world tension. The United States answers with accusations about Afghanistan and other Soviet shortcomings on détente.

Before he left office in January 1981, Edmund Muskie, who served as secretary of state during the last months of the Carter administration, said "one of the most serious challenges facing us is the continuing challenge of reading Soviet intentions." Muskie might have called it the most serious challenge in Soviet-American affairs. The problem of reading intentions led to the differing Soviet and American definitions of détente and lies at the root of the Soviet-American rivalry. And at the bottom of the problem of reading intentions is the problem of communication between the two superpowers.

The framers of détente were reaching for the right solution for Soviet-American hostility when they emphasized improved communication between the two nations at all levels. What they could not completely foresee or control was that détente itself would fall victim to the lack of communication and the problem of reading intentions. Owing to differences in national backgrounds, goals, and needs, each side misread the signals from the other, and misunderstood what the other hoped to achieve through détente. The result was renewed hostility, bitter suspicion, and a return to the cold war. We must conclude that the framework established by Nixon, Kissinger, Brezhnev, and others in the early 1970s collapsed by the late 1970s because it, too, like earlier periods of détente, was built on atmospherics, and not on substance. The fourth period of post–World War II Soviet-American détente had lasted longer than the other three, but it seemed to suffer the same fate.

POLICIES OF THE REAGAN ADMINISTRATION

In January 1981 a new administration under conservative Republican Ronald Reagan took office in Washington. Reagan had won the presidency by a landslide—in part due to his promise to restore American military strength and to improve respect for the United States abroad. During his campaign, he had attacked President Carter, accusing him of a weak and vacillating foreign policy. Reagan pledged to replace this weakness and vacillation with will, determination, and vigilance.

Very early in his administration, Reagan began to take a firm, hard line with the Soviet Union, reminiscent of earlier cold war years. At his first press conference, he declared that the only morality the Communists recognize is a morality that "will further their cause." The Communists, the President went on, "reserve unto themselves the right to commit any crime, to lie, to cheat, in order to attain" their ends. "I think when you do business with them, even in détente, you keep that in mind," he concluded.

Reagan's secretary of state, General Alexander Haig, publicly accused the Soviet Union of support for terrorist movements throughout the world and outlined a new American policy toward Russia that would stress consistency, reliability, and balance. By consistency, Haig said that he wanted the United States to abandon its policy of reacting "to events as they occur, serially, unselectively, and increasingly . . . unilaterally." This tendency, he emphasized, must be replaced with the realization that the "specific issues facing us today are merely surface manifestations of more fundamental problems." In the past, the United States had reacted to the surface events; in the future, it must try to get at the underlying problem.

By reliability, Haig explained that "American power and prestige should not be lightly committed, but once made, a commitment must be honored." In particular, he added, our allies must know that they can trust us in times of crisis. And by balance, he explained that careful priorities should be set and established, so that it is clear what issues America is most concerned about and will respond to if they arise.

Both Reagan and Haig stressed the need for increased defense spending and for dealing with the Soviet Union from a position of superiority. Neither man talked of a renewal of détente as it had been advanced in the 1970s. Some Reagan advisers spoke in favor of a new policy of containment—a policy that would freeze the Soviet empire in its present boundaries and prevent new Afghanistans. Others spoke of the need to establish joint plans with the Soviet Union for "crisis management," hoping that improved communication in times of extreme tension would improve each nation's understanding of the other's intentions. These plans, however, fell far short of détente, because they included no program of return to the Soviet-American relationship of the early seventies—no plans for increased trade and commercial ties nor for renewed scientific and cultural exchanges. It was clear that the Reagan administration wanted to review the whole spectrum of Soviet-American relations before it committed itself definitely to a new program of action.*

* Fulfilling a campaign promise made to American farmers, President Reagan ended the embargo on grain shipments to the Soviet Union. Many Washington observers regarded this move as inconsistent with the administration's hard line against the USSR. But the new President argued that the embargo had been largely ineffective and had hurt American farmers more than it had hurt the Soviet Union and therefore did not deserve to be continued.

There were two foreign policy problems, however, that the new administration had to face immediately upon taking office: Poland and El Salvador. In both of these nations, rising tensions and political difficulties that involved the interests of both East and West threatened to lead to a confrontation between Washington and Moscow. The events in Poland had begun to come to a head in the fall of 1980, with the emergence of a worker's movement, called Solidarity, that demanded and received independence from the Polish Communist party—an unheard-of situation in a Communist country where every element of society is subject to party control. Farm workers and other factions in Poland likewise displayed restlessness and pressed for demands of their own.

Across the Polish border, the Soviet Union looked upon the events in Poland with deep disapproval. Once again, as with Hungary and Czechoslovakia, Soviet leaders feared that changes in one eastern European country would lead to changes in the others and undermine Soviet authority in the area. Soviet troops were amassed on the border and threatened invasion to restore "order." How would the Reagan administration react to a Soviet attack on Poland? What policies would the United States adopt in the face of yet another act of Soviet aggression? These were the questions that faced the new President during the early days of his first term in office.

El Salvador presented another kind of problem. Located in Central America, the small but densely populated country had been engulfed in civil war for several years. The Carter administration supported a moderate government in El Salvador that had undertaken a program of land reform. But there were large and violent factions on the right and left that opposed the moderate government and resisted it with acts of terrorism and guerrilla warfare.

President Reagan continued to support the moderates, but stepped up American military aid to El Salvador in order to help the government overcome the threat from the left. Evidence taken from leftist guerrillas showed that they received support from Nicaragua, which had recently undergone a leftist revolution, from Communist Cuba, and, ultimately, from the Soviet Union. The Reagan administration looked upon El Salvador as a "test case" where American resolve to prevent Communist expansion would be verified. The problem was that many in Congress were reluctant to involve the United States in another situation that might prove to be as disastrous for America as Vietnam had been. The stage was thus set not only for a new manifestation of the rivalry between the U.S. and the USSR, but also for a contest of will between a conservative administration committed to strengthening the American position throughout the world and a political faction in Washington that viewed the revival of the cold war with dismay.

The détente of the 1970s is dead, but the need for détente lives on. The arms race continues at an increased pace and there is still no certain method to control tensions between the superpowers and to prevent major confrontations. In spite of its enormous military might, the Soviet Union still faces extreme social, political, and economic problems which only help and expertise from the advanced nations of the West can begin to solve. It may be that genuine détente is necessarily a long-term process. Perhaps the fourth period of détente, which we have discussed in this book, was merely one step, among many, that will lead eventually to a more solid understanding between the Soviet Union and the United States. It may not be too optimistic to conclude with President Kennedy's statement in his 1963 speech at American University: "Our problems are manmade, therefore they can be solved by man."

SUGGESTIONS FOR FURTHER READING

The best history of the cold war is John Lukacs, *A New History of the Cold War* (New York: Doubleday, 1966).* Also important is Adam Ulam, *Expansion and Coexistence: The History of Soviet Foreign Policy, 1917–1967* (New York: Praeger, 1968). Any of the many works of George Kennan, a Soviet expert and diplomat, are enlightening and essential.

On détente, there is Richard Barnet, *The Giants: Russia and America* (New York: Simon & Schuster, 1977),* Marshall I. Goldman, *Détente and Dollars: Doing Business with the Soviets* (New York: Basic Books, 1975), and John Newhouse, *Cold Dawn* (New York: Holt, Rinehart & Winston, 1973), an account of the negotiations leading up to SALT I.

The reader is reminded that there are several high quality magazines and journals that regularly carry articles on foreign affairs. These include *Foreign Affairs, Commentary, Orbis, The Economist,* and *The New Republic. Time,* * *Newsweek,* * and *U.S. News* and *World Report* * are also useful.

The best biography of Henry Kissinger is Bernard and Marvin Kalb, *Kissinger* (Boston: Little, Brown, 1974).

On communism and the Communist movements of recent years, see Stephen Goode, *Eurocommunism* (New York: Franklin Watts, 1980)* and *Guerrilla Warfare and Terrorism* (New York: Franklin Watts, 1977)* by the same author.

* An asterisk denotes a book or magazine that can be read with reward by a younger reader.

INDEX